Books by Ella Patterson

Will the Real Women . . . Please Stand Up!
1001 Reasons to Think Positive

Will the Real Women . . . Please Stand Up!

*Uncommon Sense About Sex,
Sensuality, and Self-Discovery*

Ella Patterson

FIRESIDE
Published by Simon & Schuster

FIRESIDE
Rockefeller Center
1230 Avenue of the Americas
New York, NY 10020

First Fireside Edition 1997

FIRESIDE and colophon are registered trademarks
of Simon & Schuster Inc.

Designed by Levavi & Levavi

Manufactured in the United States of America

7 9 10 8 6

The Library of Congress has cataloged the Simon & Schuster
edition as follows:

Patterson, Ella.
Will the real women—please stand up!
: uncommon sense about sexuality, self-esteem,
self-discovery, sex, and sensuality /
Ella Patterson.
p. cm.
Includes index.
1. Sex instruction for women—United States.
2. Women—United States—Sexual behavior.
3. Women—Health and hygiene—United States.
I. Title.
HQ46.P27 1996   96-3418 CIP

ISBN 0-684-83018-3
0-684-83151-1 (Pbk)

Acknowledgments

This book is a personal retrospection of the author; however, I attribute experiences gained during my research to many individuals. I am indebted to those friends who, over the past eight years, have knowingly and unknowingly contributed to my data. Numerous others aided generously by encouraging me to forge ahead and seek my dream. Others helped by proofreading and by expressing their ideas. They gave me honest and open criticisms.

While *Will the Real Women ... Please Stand Up!* is not a clinical treatise, my information was derived from very intensive research. My gratitude goes to various teachers, coaches, hair stylists, radio disc jockeys, college students, dentists, doctors, lawyers, and preachers for their interest and undying support.

I owe my most spirited thanks to my husband, Martin "Pig" Patterson, Jr., for his ever-present inspiration and encouragement, as well as his dedication to my venture. To my children, Juanna, T'Juanna and Martin III, I give my eternal adoration. For many reasons, my warmest thanks and undying love goes to my best friend Robert Corley and to my eternal friends Carol Murry and Marva

Owens for helping me put my thoughts onto paper. I am ever grateful to Sherylyn Jones of Salons in the Park, and Leon Fulghum of International Styles and Trends Salon of Dallas, Texas, for their personal care and attention. Special thanks to Argie Johnson, who taught me that love does last. And to my mom, Elizabeth Jones, who taught me that, no matter what, life goes on, so you might as well enjoy it. And of course, love and kisses to my oldest brother, Herbert, for his financial support and constant encouragement. I love you dearly.

To my Simon & Schuster editor, Bob Asahina, thank you for your professionalism, competence, and suggestions on this project. Your leadership and devotion have helped me grasp the insight needed to successfully complete this book. To Melissa Roberts, thanks for adorning me with your wisdom and talents.

To my literary agent, Jan Miller—we are joined at the hip. I appreciate your vision and the instincts that have contributed to my personal and professional growth. Thank you!

And lastly, I give thanks to God, who in Jesus' name gave me the strength to do the research and the ever-present courage to write this book, along with the endurance to seek and find women willing to talk to me openly about their sexuality. And God, please let Oprah Winfrey read my book!

This one's for . . .
All those women who have taught me
that life goes on.

Contents

The mind forgets,
but the heart always remembers,
that love does last.

—A.E.J.

Will the Real Women . . . Please Stand Up!

Introduction: Why a Book Like This?

 T his is a book that separates the women from the girls. This is a no-holds-barred book—straight to the point—with a true look at commonsense female sexuality and sensuality. This is a book that deals with the real issues that women face in sexuality throughout their lives. This is a book that says all the things that women have been afraid to say, and it answers many questions that women may have been too embarrassed to ask.

I suggest that women read this book with an open mind. Any woman can open the doors of sensuality and sexual satisfaction if she opens up her mind and rids herself of "nice girls don't do that" type of thinking. It's been said that most men want a woman who is:

- more than beautiful
- more than brilliant
- more than a good housekeeper
- more than a good mother to his children

Most men want a multitalented and sensuously mature woman. Sensuously mature women make men feel more loved and more cared for. Through observation, manipulation, concentration, and exploration, you too can accomplish the how-tos of erotic pleasures that await you and your lover. Each turn of the page will open your eyes to why a book like this is needed and is so important to all real women. Real Women want to please their men in rich, rewarding, and nurturing ways. Real Women must therefore take a stand and finally discover their own sexuality and sexual capabilities. A Real Woman must take the necessary steps toward pleasing her man sexually. In return, he will take care of all of her needs, wants, and desires.

Will the Real Women . . . Please Stand Up! is a compilation of sensual and sexual issues that women encounter throughout their sexually active lives. True sensuality is not a compilation of *cut-and-dried* facts; rather, it is an account of fascinating secrets, solutions, and games for contemporary women. In addition, this book presents women with choices, pleasures, entertainments, and optimistic commonsense on sexual freedoms.

Before we begin this journey of sensual and sexual freedom, I'd like to explain just how I came to write a book like this.

Upon graduation from college, I received teaching certifications in health, physical education, history, and biology. I later taught in the Dallas Independent School District as a health, biology, psychology, sociology, and history teacher, and as a coach for a total of fourteen years. After deciding to get recertified in health education, I became aware of a need to train people newly arrived from other countries in the basic hygiene practiced in the United States. I was informed by a supervisor at the health department that hotels were looking for such a person during the summer months. I set out to develop a company to help people from foreign countries adjust to lifestyles and conditions in the United States. I discovered that such a company did not in fact exist. Little did I know that the development of these hygiene classes would later create a desire to investigate and write about the concerns of women.

I began offering hygiene classes to the hotel chains. I developed a letter of introduction, made a thousand copies of it, and mailed them off to hotels both near and far. The response was minimal but I didn't stop there. I knew the need existed, so I figured that my approach needed an upgrade. I developed a brochure to send along with my letter of introduction, a brochure that was appealing, interesting, and helpful.

In 1993, in the midst of my excitement to speak to others about health issues, I was in a terrible car accident. I took a sick leave from my teaching job. While recuperating, I became restless, bored, and agitated. My doctor sent me to physical therapy to regain my strength, but that did not cure my boredom. I wanted to go back to work. The doctor asked me what I liked to do most. I told him I enjoyed writing. "Then that's your prescription," he said. "You can't go back to work yet, but you can write." So as part of my therapy I began to write.

As my subject, I decided to write about women's issues. But in order for me to write about women's issues, I had to talk to women— real women. I had to talk to women of all races, creeds, colors, and backgrounds in order to make this project a success. I didn't want to learn everything from books, I wanted firsthand information from women who would be willing to talk to me about their own stories of feminine hygiene.

As I began to speak to women of all nationalities, I set out to train myself on the who, what, where, how, and when of things. I needed to know the proper way to speak about hygiene, cleanliness, and female maintenance without offending women from other cultures. While all this was going on, I began to receive calls from some of the hotels to which I had sent introductory letters. I was now in business. Other groups and organizations began to call. Although my tiny business began to flourish, I still felt I needed to do more. I decided that since I had presented a brochure, the time had come for me to create a book with my seminar information. I chose to focus my company by naming it Knowledge Concepts Educational Systems. I wanted people to know that my company addressed issues that others were afraid to tackle.

Once again I began to interview women to become better informed on the customs and curiosities of people from other places. The more women I interviewed, the more I wanted to know. I wanted to know, and I asked women *why some of them felt that their needs were not being met*. From this question, I received an enormous response. This question single-handedly paved the way for women to talk openly and honestly about hygiene, sex, sexuality, sexual organs, douching, cleansing, personal appearance, solitude, body balance, and much, much more.

Time was an issue. I needed diversity. I needed to find more women from all cultures to interview. In order to complete my research I had to find a place where hundreds of women gathered for long periods of time. I knew that I couldn't afford to travel all over the world, so I had to come up with the next best thing. Suddenly it hit me: The Apparel Mart, the Trade Mart, and the Market Hall. What better place in Dallas to find women of all races, creeds, colors, and economic backgrounds. "There is a God!" I screamed, as the idea came to me.

But the challenge had just begun. Now I had to find a way to get into these places to talk to women. The Apparel Mart, the Trade Mart, and the Market Hall are all off limits to the general public. The first day I sneaked in—with pen and paper in hand—through a side door with a group of women merchandisers from Neiman Marcus. For approximately twenty-seven days I sneaked in this way until I finally got caught by one of the security guards. I knew I was wrong, so I graciously walked out, escorted by two guards. I wasn't finished yet! The next day, I walked right in through the front door and began to interview female security guards in order to get past them without any question. After about twenty minutes, I told them that I had to complete my interviews and I waved goodbye. They helped me to get to where I was trying to go without even knowing it. They were so happy to be interviewed that they volunteered to escort me to my next interview. Of course, I assured them that I could handle it, because at that point I had no idea who I was going to interview next! After about seventy-five more interviews that day, I decided to get a snack. On my way, I bumped into one of the guards who had put me out of the building the day before. The guard pointed me to the nearest exit. As I walked down the sidewalk, one of the guards who had escorted me out the day before said, "Why don't you just do the right thing?" I said, "Okay" and went on my way. Three weeks of research had passed and I was a little tired of the hassles. So I began to think of new strategies to help me get more interviews.

I rode around in my car for hours thinking of places where I could find women willing to talk to me hassle-free. Finally, I went home and began to sort out the material I had collected. I had so much information that it was very difficult to decide exactly how I was going to use it. Most of it was so detailed and so open that I felt it was a bit *too real* for the general public. Just then the idea hit me to write two books: one on hygiene; the other on real issues, real women, and the concerns of all women. I prepared five sample chapters in book form and decided to distribute them to people waiting on line at movie theaters. After all, waiting in line is one of the most boring things to do, so I decided to provide people with a little reading material to keep them occupied. I visited the local movie theaters on weekends, and gave bound sample chapters away as part of my research to see what people thought about my creating a book like this.

I greeted people at the theaters with a verbal introduction. My introduction went something like this: "Hi! My name is Ella Patterson. I'm the author of the new book, *Will the Real Women . . . Please Stand Up!* I'd like to give you a sample copy of my book. Would you please take a little of your time to read it? If you don't like it, throw it away. If you like it, please feel free to call the toll-free telephone number on the back of this sample and give me your personal opinions and/or views. If you have any suggestions on how I could improve this research, I would love to hear them."

Within two days I began to receive telephone calls. These calls were not quite what I expected. Instead of comments and advice, I began to receive orders for my book. A book that was not yet written! The orders were coming in by the hundreds. That's when I knew I had hit on something; yet I wasn't prepared to fill any orders because I was still in the middle of the research phase. I had to continue to gather information for my book, and I needed more opinions from more women of different cultures.

So I was back to the beginning. I had to come up with another way to get into the Dallas Trade Mart, the Apparel Mart, and the Market Hall without being thrown out. My plan was to get an identification badge that I had seen other people wearing. I drove to the front door this time, parked my car, and proceeded to the front desk to find out how I could obtain legal entry. I was told that if I had a business with a tax exempt number I could get in. All I had was my business card, which was insufficient. I had never obtained a tax exempt number. After seeking information on how to get one, I headed for the door. Time was of the essence. As I turned to walk away, I noticed an outdated badge lying on a countertop unattended and unclaimed. I took it home and put in on my scanner, duplicated it, put my name on it with my computer, and laminated my new badge with my laminating machine. I headed back to the Dallas Apparel Mart to test it out.

I greeted the security guards at the door, showed them my badge, and walked right in. I had made it past the first obstacle; the true test would begin when I entered the shops to talk to the women. Everything worked like a charm, and I interviewed over seven thousand women for this book.

The women I interviewed were between the ages of fifteen and seventy-nine. These women talked openly about sensuality and the sensitive side of their sexuality. I discovered many amazing things about many women throughout my research. All women have sexual secrets, motives, dreams, beliefs, and desires. What classifies them as real women is purely a matter of opinion.

These women revealed that the majority of them don't confer with one another with the intent to spread gossip. They merely talked to one another to learn so that they could experiment or try new things on their own partners. Many described ways to incorporate sensuous spice, add adventurous allure, bring teasing tantalization, and become pleasingly provocative as they sensuously welcomed sexuality in relationships whether culturally acceptable or unacceptable. Many women didn't allow society to determine their sexual practices.

The women I interviewed also told me of their need to achieve orgasms with or without intercourse. Orgasms were a matter of priority for most women. Women who experienced masturbation enjoyed it, and clitoral stimulation was a big issue with almost every one of them. However, *Will the Real Women . . . Please Stand Up!* is not just a sex manual. It is about complete sensuality. It describes basic hygiene and numerous ways to use knowledge of sensuality to stimulate your mate. It does so without reducing wholesome sexual pleasures to a list of statistics and manual stimulations. This book is filled with suggestions, games, and erotic techniques. But it should be remembered that these are only suggestions toward complete female sensuality, and nothing more. If there are any practices that violate your personal sexual code of ethics, skip them and try others. It is your right to reject any of them as well as experience the pleasures of some of them. Some games may be especially appealing to you and your partner. As always, you may want to incorporate your own methods with those suggested.

So the simple idea to create a brochure for my company's hygiene presentations helped create the book that you are now reading. Enjoy yourself, and try not to create barriers that will exclude you from further sensuous explorations. Patterns have been known to create boredom. Not all entries in this book are sexual, but all will help to validate and add something special to your relationship. This book is the starting point for your newfound sexual happiness.

Happy sexuality!

1

Becoming a Real Woman

❧ What It's Going to Take ❧

You're about to change your life. Inside this book you'll find everything you've ever needed to know about being a Real Woman but were afraid to ask. It's all here for you: the most current sexual trends; money-saving ideas to please you and to satisfy your man; tricks of the trade that everyone will want to know. In this book you'll find the secrets of how successful women turn their men on. Your personal confidence level will rise to heights of complete, positive acceptance, and you'll do the right things to be the total woman in business as well as in bed. Whoever said that business and pleasure don't mix was probably a dull fuck who wasn't handling sex and business in an appropriate way. The reality of your being a Real Woman is only a thought away. It's time for women to do the right thing by enjoying love, life, sex, and the pursuit of happiness in the bedroom without feeling shame or guilt. This book is for those who claim to be Real Women, and those who someday want to be.

In so many wonderful, positive, and rewarding ways this book will help you to:

- find men
- meet men
- seduce men
- go on a diet and keep the inspiration to stay on it
- attain fabulous breasts from those you already possess
- select the most sensuous lingerie without losing the support you need
- wear sensuous shoes: from bedroom slippers to tennis shoes to high heels
- be the queen of his night and the lady of his wet dreams
- dress seductively without looking like a tramp
- kiss very sensuously and not tell
- get more of what you want from men
- have women at your feet and not be lesbian
- remain romantic in and out of bed
- sexually stimulate with every part of your sensuous body
- be sensuous and not be considered sleazy

I've been listening to women complain about what their men want, what their men aren't doing to satisfy them, and how they want to turn their men on more. I've read every book on sex and relationships that's been printed for the past fifteen years, and they all seem to say the same things. They say enough of what we want to hear but not enough of what we really need to know. My book is concerned with what *all* women want and need to know about complete female sensuality.

I am a wife/mother/friend/teacher/coach/author/business-woman and now professional speaker extraordinaire. Through my many talents I've had many opportunities to learn. My years of good tips, trials, and tribulations have made me an authority on sensuous street savvy and romance. There is an art to being a contemporary woman of vision with sensuous attributes.

The ingredients to be this woman of vision with an adventurous spirit are the keys to unlocking the complexities of a *Real Woman*. And only a woman can do that. I was born and raised in East St. Louis, Illinois. In a short time, I learned the ropes of self-marketing, the magic of being a good listener, the value of true friendship, the ups and downs of media support, and the blessings that come with knowing how to pray. Since I'm of Irish descent, I give luck plenty of credit too.

I've always been told to know the rules, but I've found out that not knowing all of the rules has many advantages. Whether I'm at work or at home, with friends or with lovers, from nightlife to day life, I follow my guidelines of sensuality. The way to a man's heart is through his woman, and the way to a woman's heart is through her man. Each must have something unique to offer the other in a positive, beneficial, and exciting manner. After all, nothing is free, not even the love you think you give so freely. I'll get more into lover's benefits later in this book.

The purpose of this book is to share my knowledge with you. My sincere objective is to bring to you the things that absolutely turn men on. I will give to you the things that women have told me about love, happiness, relationships, sex, and fulfillment in life. Being a sexy, interesting, romantic, open-minded, and confident woman in all situations is only partially the scope of this book. I'll show you how to have fun in life by taking your best attributes of being a woman and fusing them with strength, independence, self-esteem, intelligence, etiquette, and confidence. You'll be able to enjoy your sexiness as you confidently adore men and still feel beautiful as you are given love. You will begin to notice a difference in how you look, how you feel, and how you think about yourself. Your personal effectiveness and how you communicate with others will improve. So become diligent and get ready to love the new you.

❧⊱⊰❧

Bring knowledge to your mind.

❧⊱⊰❧

2

Getting Prepared

*T*ake your copy of *Will the Real Women . . . Please Stand Up!* and find a quiet, comfortable, and secluded place to read. Get your favorite drink; it doesn't necessarily have to be alcoholic, just as long as it's your favorite. Find your favorite loungewear, get comfortable, and snuggle up until you feel cozy. Take the phone off the hook, and if you have to send the entire family to the movies for a few hours or so, do it.

As you begin to read *Will the Real Women . . . Please Stand Up!*, allow no distractions to interfere with the learning process. You are about to wake up to a whole new, exciting, motivated, vibrant, and fulfilling mental awareness. We'll name this area your Sensuous Zone. Some of the discoveries in this book will allow you to use the sensuous thinking of your brain. Once these sensuous centers are awakened, many doors will be opened, unexpected doors. When these doors begin to open and create this wonderful sensitivity, so will the possibilities of a more fulfilling existence.

❧ *Preparing Your Environment*

Your environment must include you. The mood should exemplify a pleasant and welcome invitation. It should be clean and it should represent your personal self. Your environment will include the people who are going to make love, so it should have a wholesome atmosphere. To make love in a bed with cracker crumbs or dirty linens is not healthy nor inviting. Give your lover a reason to be taken to your bed other than for sex. A clean and fresh environment is the first step toward a clean and healthy association. If your partner knows that you're clean, he'll work to present a clean and healthy relationship as well.

Placing romantic scents and beautiful linens in your bedroom will send out pleasant signals to your special guest. Many women have found that a clean and fresh-smelling living environment is a major asset.

Getting rid of all the dingy bed linens—those with holes, stains, torn, or full of lint balls—and putting new ones on your bed can make you feel more sensuous when slipping between the sheets. When washing your bed linens use fabric softener and a small amount of lingerie soap to enhance the aroma as well as soften the texture. These additions to what you already have will add romance and sensuality. Aromatic candles create scents as well as special effects.

❧

*To have power, you must be clear
on what you want.*

❧

3

Getting the Man You Want

◆◆ Proven Techniques ◆◆

*T*he best way to land a lover is to become totally and irresistibly attractive to him. You're going to have to be warm, attentive, attractive, and you must carry a permanent glow on the inside and out.

Before you go any further, you must know the answers to a few questions.

- Does the man of your dreams possess the qualities that you feel are satisfactory?
- Does he have generosity as well as integrity?

Men who aren't generally generous with their resources won't be generous with their love, affection, and caring. Generosity depends on the man involved. Many men who are wealthy aren't necessarily generous. Some men are generous with their time, some are generous with their advice, and some are generous with their sex. The generosity that's being focused on here is *spirit*.

Generosity is the time he makes available for whenever and

whatever your needs. And for you to be just as generous to him is worth the giving. Knowing what you need as a woman is great, but knowing what you want in a man is fantastic. Be sure you know what qualities you seek in a man and then be just as sure the man you select possesses these qualities.

A woman can find ways to seek out the qualities she wants in a man. Whatever that most important quality is, find it. Expect it and then demand it. Don't cheat yourself. Expect the best for yourself by expecting what you want as a woman. Expecting these qualities in the man you've chosen is not being selfish, it's being sure of what you want in a man and that means not to settle for less. Your happy life starts with you, and as a woman, your happiness is your number one priority. Here are some proven techniques to help you get the man you want.

1. BE ATTENTIVE TO HIM

Focus all your attention on the man you want. Become so genuinely engrossed in what he's saying that everything else disappears. Be able to look him right in the eye and give him your complete concentration. Making him feel that he's the most brilliant man you've ever met is the key.

2. LEARN TO BE CONVERSANT

Men like to talk about themselves. So you've got to be able to ask questions that will make him want to go on and on about himself. Winning questions consist of snoop questions. You might be bored with his likes and dislikes, but you've got to overcome your selfishness and focus in on what makes him tick. What makes him tick is you being in awe of him. Don't think of it as being nosy either; use good judgment on what you ask and practice the art of conversation. Start with something simple, like his business or his hobbies. What's his favorite vacation spot or his favorite food? Ask personal questions that aren't intimidating, like what's his favorite movie, or what's his least favorite food. Even questions such as, "Do you still have your favorite childhood toy?" can spark an interesting conversation.

Remember to look him straight in the eyes as you talk to him;

this will bring out those things he always wanted to tell but didn't think anyone wanted to hear. He'll love it and he'll love you even more for being interested enough to let him brag about himself.

3. Don't Be Afraid to Flatter Him

Self-esteem and inner strength aren't listed as finer qualities in men. Men may look strong on the exterior, but their interiors are weaker than the most delicate women. Men need to be told that they are beautiful and that they are great in bed. Get in the habit of telling your man that you find him irresistible and gorgeous. Most women find it exhilarating and challenging to offer compliments to a man. For those men who need to be complimented or reassured, be especially attentive to them. Don't get caught up in flattery by telling lies. Compliments that are lies hurt people in the long run. They know when a lie is a lie on most occasions. Don't you?

4. Be Available

Playing hard to get has its virtues, but don't entertain this idea for too long a period unless there's a reason for it. Be available, supportive, and never play too hard to get. Saying no to a man too soon can be premature. A man generally wants to show a woman that he cares, so when he asks you to join him don't be so quick to say no. Don't hold yourself back. Learn new things by not joining the hard-to-get club. Men enjoy women who are available. Being available does not mean doing things that you don't like. It simply means learning new things with the man you've chosen. Having the right attitude will display the character and principles that are needed to prove your own tastes, and this alone will improve your self-esteem. You don't have to be a snob by constantly saying "no, or not this time." Sharing in his life in a positive and rewarding way will help him to miss you when you're not around.

5. Continue to Have Fun

Sometimes he won't be able to assist you or accommodate you and you'll be disappointed about it. Make your needs attractive to him by sharing the fun. By this I mean, if you like to go to the movies and he'd rather stay home and watch old reruns, compromise. Why don't you rent his favorite movie that you also like and, without forcing him to go out to the movies, enjoy a romantic evening and top it with his favorite dessert . . . *you*. The compromise can be worthwhile if it becomes something both of you can enjoy. Turn your fun into spicy enchantment. Keeping his needs in mind can be fun, and in return he'll begin to focus in on your needs because you'll be the one in charge.

6. BE WHAT HE LIKES IN A WOMAN

Being straightforward with your man and asking him what he likes can open many doors of pleasures between the two of you. If he knows you like him and you treat him better than any other woman, he'll like you more. If a man knows a woman desires him, she becomes more desirable to him. Never be scared to show him that you desire him. Let him know that you desire his warmth and affection. Touch him as often as you possibly can; stroke his sideburns. And if he doesn't have any, stroke his face. Men will respond to these gestures in a positive way. They love this kind of contact. Extending warmth and demonstrative touching doesn't have to be sexual. Any woman or man of quality knows the difference between warmth and sexual aggression. Men adore human touch because it shows the affection they so badly miss and need. If a woman is self-confident, warm, and caring, men will be attracted to her. Men also cherish a woman with something to give, a woman who is comfortable with herself. Remember, to get what you want, you sometimes have to ask for it.

7. BE FAMILIAR WITH LIFE'S PLEASURES

Convey a combination of glamour, happiness, and directness. Being blunt and feminine at the same time is found to be provocative to men. Don't be afraid to say what's on your mind to the man you're interested in. Clear-speaking and confident-talking women are sexy to men. Women who are familiar with life's pleasures are in control of their own pleasures. A woman who isn't afraid to let her man know what she wants or likes is an enticing feature. Men seem to find it a real turn on. Some men don't like to play games, and when they find a woman who's as strong as they are, it is an accomplishment. Men think that when a woman speaks plainly of her wants, needs, and desires it shows that she doesn't play games.

Being direct is a sign of loyalty, and men look for loyalty in their partners. Having a woman they can count on is a plus in any relationship. Make your man the center of your attention by allowing him the opportunity to be the center of your desire. Then show him how big your desires are.

8. Sex Shouldn't Be a Condition of Pleasures

Don't ever have sex unless you want to, and don't give in to sex until you want it. If you tell him no and he tries to add conditions to your answer, let him go. A woman can control her own agenda, and if the man doesn't like it, so what. A man cannot be kept, held, or loved any longer by giving in to his sexual requests when you don't want to have sex. Sex isn't the ultimate of what a man wants from a woman. His commitment comes from his interest in you as a woman; sex is an addition to this interest. Morals and self-respect can help your judgment in making important decisions about sex. Your decisions about sex should be pleasurable, and you should feel good about yourself and about your relationship before sex enters the picture. He'll value you more if you aren't easily accessible or available sexually.

9. Don't Sweat the Small Stuff

Don't get caught up into arguing about the small stuff. In any relationship, you will have big and small experiences that neither of you will always agree upon. A rule to always remember: "Don't sweat the small stuff." Rule number two: "It's all small stuff." All relationships are give and take. There will be times when you'll have to give in, and there will be times when he'll have to give in. Don't keep a tally of who gives in the most or the least. Make compromises by taking turns selecting the activity for the day, week, or month. What's considered big stuff and what's considered the little stuff are different for all of us. Having the ability to make the distinction is what separates the women from the girls. It's really a matter of mature opinions on most occasions. Just because you give in to your man doesn't mean that your womanhood is compromised. Having the power to compromise and feel confident about your decision is a step in the right direction.

10. ENJOY GOING OUT ALONE

The chances of meeting someone you'll like is always greater when you go out rather than when you just sit at home. The need to have a man with you every time you go out can be discouraging for an interested fellow. Going out with married friends can open up many possibilities of meeting men who are looking for a new adventure with someone just like you. Tagging along can be a new experience and, who knows, you might just meet your better half.

❧❧❧

Know what it takes to make you happy.

❧❧❧

4

Finding Him

❧ Where to Meet Men ❧

As a sensuous woman, you're not looking for just any man. You're looking for a certain type of man, a man who will turn you on physically, emotionally, and intellectually. Be realistic in the mental image you create of your ideal mate. While creating this image, picture the type of man who will be attracted to you.

Be honest and give yourself a critical self-evaluation. In today's society it is considered more acceptable for a woman to go hunting for the man she wants. Men have always been entitled to pursue women who have attracted their attention. Even though some women prefer to be chased and seduced, situations do occur that allow women to become more aggressive in the hunt. To keep from becoming overly aggressive, a woman must manipulate her prey before he will completely appreciate how much she yearns for him.

Men have an extraordinary lack of self-confidence when it comes to meeting new women. Men with inflated egos who believe they are attractive to all women are still around. Usually they act shy, or tongue-tied, or too macho, or overboastful, or they lean over backwards to impress.

It takes a mature and confident gentleman to enjoy, without personal judgment, a direct approach from a mature and confident woman. A woman must first know in her own mind what she wants in a man as well as what she wants from a man. Some women want regular meals in the finest restaurants, rides in the classiest cars, and fur coats of the highest quality. There are rich men with no looks who would be glad to provide these luxuries. There are also men with great looks who would be equally happy to provide these luxuries. My rule is to never criticize gold diggers, because every woman has a right to be happy whether financially or physically.

Society today encourages give and take, and supply and demand, so a woman should give her man what he wants and then he'll let her take as much as she wants. She should supply her man with what he wants and then demand what she needs. A man loves the idea of having a sensuous, sensitive, and beautiful woman on his arm and in his bed. And I have found through research and observation that he's usually willing to pay the price to get her.

❦

*The greatest secret of women who win
is persistence.*

❦

5

Playing His Game

Women want reasonably handsome men with personality, integrity, and love along with plenty of material possessions. When a woman finally finds the man she's been waiting for, she should allow him to feel as though he did the picking and the choosing. Don't give any hints or signs that he's been picked out by you. He'll love a hint of rejection, so don't make yourself too available for him. Keep a balance between acceptance and rejection. Go back and forth until he's confused with desire. Practice giving yourself, and allow it to become a natural reflex. Flirt politely with the warmth of a smile and a welcome glance at all potential prey. Approximately 45 percent will flirt back.

Smile often and glance regularly at men who have attracted your attention. Focus on each one for about two or three seconds or more. Narrow down those who continue to flirt with you to your personal finalist. Find those whose eyes are watching you, trying to flirt with you, and then focus in on your chosen targets. The guys who continue to flirt and remain in your presence are your best picks. Choose one and flirt directly with him. Remain discreet so as not to discourage the others, just in case this one doesn't work out for you. Flirt intensely and consistently, but don't give him all of your time, and by all means don't monopolize all of his time.

To assure yourself a few good picks, flirt with the others in the same fashion, and then narrow your choices to the number one pick. Remember that you are doing the picking and choosing without his knowing it. This will build your confidence level to maximum heights, yet his male ego will remain intact because he'll think he did the picking.

Okay. You've made your choice, but suppose he's married or involved in a happy relationship with another woman? Then you'll have to be strong and you'll have to make some important decisions. If he wants to have an affair with you, you will have to remember and understand that he has obligations and responsibilities that will take priority over you.

Asking him to leave his family, home, and wife won't put you on his most wanted list. Emotions are human and most men would rather have an affair than pay the price for leaving. Many people automatically blame the other woman, but few men are naturally monogamous and many must have more than one woman to feel satisfied. Entering into an affair with a married man can be painful if you go in blinded. To enjoy this affair be prepared to enjoy the best but also expect the worst.

❧❧❧

Remind yourself that you are a valuable,
worthwhile human being.

❧❧❧

6

Winning Techniques

Men lack confidence. So, if you're interested in one, you'd better send out obvious signals of your attraction or he'll miss them all. In a room full of people (mainly men), one of the best seduction techniques is to scan the room and then flirtatiously go for what you know.

Stare frequently at your choice. And with each stare, lengthen its duration. Short glances and small encouraging smiles have terrific effects on men. Men usually eye women, so turning the tables flatters them tremendously. Lingering, sly looks allow you to show interest without committing yourself. It will open the way for him to approach you and start a conversation. Don't get all wild and slaver over him when he displays a coolness. Drop a hint of your interest every now and then so he won't lose his nerve and decide not to talk to you. Even if he seems to be unsure, give him a chance. He'll show you his appreciation with great responses.

To make an extra impression on the man you've chosen, provoke an intelligent argument after listening to him for a while. Nothing gets a man's adrenaline flowing faster than a woman who can argue intelligently and seductively. Don't get too worked up or too excited or too overbearing. Keep your cool and be pleasantly contradictory. You'll find that he's suddenly giving you all of his attention, that he's found an excitement while talking to you. You'll find that you've become a challenge that he doesn't find in other women, and he'll give extra effort with you.

The stage is now set for challenge, reaction, attraction, and seduction. Men are obviously flattered by women who answer to their every beck and call, but they're intrigued and turned on by women who won't. Your openness in the way you approach men is up to you, but be ready to back up whatever you do or say. If you get overly aggressive with a man don't scream wolf if he wants to fuck you. He's only responding to your gestures. Don't lead a man on and don't let him think you're an easy lay. You'll end up physically abused or emotionally torn. Resist laughing too loudly when you're surrounded by a host of men. Men will not see you as sexy or attractive, they will see you as silly.

Women who attract men regularly are women who look fantastic, encouraging, promising, sexy, and distinctively different with something in reserve. The woman who has secrets is the woman with something that arouses men to a challenge. She'll be the one who's sexy without being overbearing or a nymphomaniac. She'll be vocal without being too outspoken, and she'll know when to open her seductive eyes, close her mouth, and listen to one of his ego-tripping tales.

A man loves a woman who listens to his stories of himself and his personal achievements. It helps to build his ego when he tells stories of his rejections. Be positive and stroke his ego when he's showing signs of low self-esteem.

Regularly compliment him, and as you do, stroke his back slightly; this will give him goose bumps. Stroke his sideburns while saying nice things. If you smoke, gently hold his wrist as he lights your cigarette. You can also pretend to read his palm as you gently stroke his hand. This will send messages of comfort throughout his body. Stimulating a man can be quite simple if you use creativity and imagination.

Dancing can bring about hidden seductiveness also. Dancing gives women an excuse to be seductive, just as respectability can be achieved from clinging on his arm. A woman can grind, roll, touch, and moan without anyone knowing. She can masturbate him and dance with him at the same time. She can use her thighs when dancing and cause him to have an erection.

You don't have to be a whore to be attracted to a man you want but don't know. In a busy store, airport, or grocery you can have a man help you choose deodorants, colognes, or even shaving creams by asking for his help in your selections. Asking him to sniff wrists, arms, necks, of even your hair is a great turn on for him.

If you see a stranger and you are attracted to him, be very subtle and ask where you might buy a hat or any other piece of clothing he is wearing—for your brother. Other tactics are to ask directions, the time, or something brief that needs a lengthy explanation. He'll notice that you're a good listener.

When using these techniques you are still left your dignity; you aren't being pushy and overbearing. The actual invitation will appear to be his, and the fun of it all is that he doesn't realize he's been set up to react a certain way.

Many women believe that cooking a four-course meal is the way to get the man she wants. In reality, what will get her the man is confidence in herself as a woman. Letting him know you want him will get a better response than a candlelit dinner. Stealing time to cook and prepare a meal for him takes time away from valuable intimacy. Besides, you're likely to drive him away; men think women are looking for a husband when they prepare elaborate dinners for two. Be sure you're tidy, warm, cordial, and, most of all, feminine. Keep a couple of bottles of wine and a nice bottle of liquor around. Have pizza, Chinese food, or cheese and crackers or even finger foods, but don't overdo it on food. You want him and he wants you, not your food. Dressing sexy is best when you are trying to romance your man. A frilly, low-cut blouse and a long, tight skirt will work. Wearing no under garments is nice and sexy too. Tight slacks with a glittery tank top are provocative. Be sure hair and makeup are fresh and always complimentary. Invest in kinky underwear for later in the relationship to heighten sensuality.

Early in the relationship, play the sexy, desirable, innocent girl; not the experienced woman ready for mad sex. Do everything to make him comfortable. Don't go to the bathroom to finish your makeup and tell him to fix his own drink. Remain in his presence, hang up his jacket, and pour him his drink. Ask if he would like something to eat and if he says no don't let it bother you. Keep the mood relaxed and positive.

Once you've done everything that's needed to assure he's com-

fortable, you can relax. Now that both of you are relaxed, let the relationship begin.

With these winning techniques you're going to be the apple of several men's eyes, so be ready to enjoy pampering and let the feelings
flow. The men I interviewed said that they appreciate women who
are sure of themselves, and not overbearing or cocky. This doesn't
mean you should be so submissive that you begin to feel like
his slave. No one wants a mate who is a sucker for love. It doesn't
help either person's self-esteem, nor does it increase the passion.
Being a puppet is not being considerate or in love. Men might adore
your whining and helpless attitude in the beginning of a relationship
because of their ego, but after a few weeks of this he'll soon tire and
begin to look for a woman who has it more together. Most men want
women who can carry their own weight and still connect with their
femininity. They are also attracted to women who do not appear to
be a future handicap to their checkbook or their time. And don't forget those little emergency items in your purse. These gadgets and
handy tools can serve your needs as well as his. I've listed a few
things to help you get it all together.

Miniature flashlights can be purchased at hardware stores.
Pepper spray can be purchased at gas stations, car dealerships,
    and some grocery stores.
Handkerchiefs.
Mirror that is tiny and easy to pack in your purse.
Tweezers to stay ahead of the unwanted hair game.
Fingernail clippers.
A small notepad should be a natural part of your attire so you
    can take down numbers or to send little notes to a man that
    you admire from afar.
Small purses are attractive and feminine as well as conservative
    on a beautifully dressed woman.
Breath mints and toothbrush and toothpaste for freshening your
    breath.
Extra panties are a girl's best friend—you can leave a pair for
    him to sniff after you've gone, or you'll have a fresh pair to
    change into when needed throughout an active day.
Small, delicate gadgets of your personal choice are also handy:
    miniature pens or pencils, key lights, perfume samples, ear-
    rings.

❧ Special Note

Don't let your items become too bulky or noisy. No Real Woman needs to attract unnecessary attention by clinging and clanging on her entrance. Your items must be subtle and slightly noticeable. Take only those items that *really* serve a purpose—that should help to narrow your list down.

❧❧❧

Shine, even if the sun doesn't.

❧❧❧

7

Becoming a Sensuous Woman

After years of research, I have found that some of the most confusing and disappointing experiences of women have been sensual or sexual.

Some of my most tantalizing, earthshaking, shrieking, faint-inducing moments have been sexual. Once you have had your first sexual encounter, it becomes an inescapable part of joy. Who we are sexually is something we learn throughout our lives.

We, as women, owe it to ourselves to understand our own sexuality, sensuality, sexual needs, and desires. To begin to understand why it's so important to be a sensuous woman, I've covered several topics that I've found to be the most beneficial. After talking to hundreds of women about sexuality, I've found that all of them have one thing in common when it comes to the men they love: Women try to keep their men by pleasing them ultimately.

To be sensuous does not mean to be weak; however, to be soft and fragile is a necessity. You must appear to enjoy the role of the so-called weaker sex. The luxury of having doors opened, chairs pulled out, packages carried, and being able to cry openly when we feel like it is a natural part of being a woman. The benefits of sensuality can sometimes be very rewarding. The joy of giving everything of ourselves to the men we love, and the delight of receiving great gifts like diamonds, minks, and rubies are all rewards for succeeding in sensuality.

You can consider yourself lucky if you already possess sensuous qualities. Every woman should have the chance to discover her sensuous self. So go ahead, enjoy yourself in bed, have orgasms, lots of them. And don't go through guilt trips afterward. Women are now realizing for the first time that they are not just receptacles for sperm. Our bodies are *not* just a place to store embryos.

Good lovemaking should become the number one priority with you and your man. Good lovemaking awakens you emotionally, spiritually, and sensuously by relaxing your mind, body, and spirit.

Enjoy the sensuous aspects of lovemaking, because it makes you forget your worries for a while. It aids in attaining restful sleep and is one of the *oldest* pleasures in this world.

In sensuous lovemaking, you will not be alone. Your companion should be someone who is compassionate, sensitive, and admiring, who wants to give and take you completely to new sexual heights. You can get all the loving that's needed if you unwrap your sensuality. Work with every ounce of your being to make things work in your favor. Don't deprive yourself unnecessarily, because you can change your negative sexual and emotional patterns. I have, and I've found a happiness that has long been awaited.

Some of us come into full sexuality without effort. For most women, however, becoming a completely sensuous woman is often a difficult process. In the past, very few have succeeded. But with this book and a desire to learn, your success rate will increase. As women, we owe this to ourselves.

If you are not sensuous, you are cheating yourself and you need to know it. Don't frustrate yourself by blaming anyone. Be sensuous by loving your body and enjoying who you are. Be sensuous by being smart and aware of who you are. Be sensuous with your actions. Think, walk, and speak sensuous, and most of all, look discreetly sensuous.

By achieving the correct response patterns, the sensuality within you will come pouring out, yet remain reserved. In other words, your sensuousness will show; it will be used in a positive way and remain intact to be used over and over again on the men of your choice.

To become sensuous and remain sensuous, women must practice

their sensuality techniques on a daily basis. In these times, women of all ages can be sensuous. Unleashing the pent-up passion that's been waiting to be freed is the first step. Forget the myths of nice girls don't do that. I've been told more than once by guys of all ages that men want a nice young lady. Yes, a nice young lady, but with whorelike qualities. Every man wants a fantastic bed partner without inhibitions and hang-ups. Executives, schoolteachers, secretaries, lawyers, doctors, therapists, and others can all be good girls by everyone's standards, but to her man she needs to be the good little whore. So go on, girls, be a whore for your man, and a very good one too. Catch fire, concentrate on sex, think of your satisfaction, and climax with your lover. When the sensuality of it all sets in, you will feel much more secure as a woman, and a sensuous woman at that.

"Hmmm," I thought, if this program works for me, then why wouldn't it work for all women? I began a few test cases, like my best friend, Larna. Larna met a lot of men but could never seem to keep them interested in her. They always left after three or four weeks. I set out to find the problem. After a few weeks of girl talk and comparisons of her dates, I found that she was only going out with men who she thought had money. That was okay, but why did they leave so quickly? One problem that needed fixing was that once Larna got the man she wanted, she had to learn how to keep him. We began my "Will the Real Women . . . Please Stand Up" program. She found that my program enabled her to keep her lovers coming back for more. Each time they came (smile), they left fulfilled, and she reaped the rewards and awards sexually, physically, mentally, and financially.

❧

Women enjoy the happiness they give.
Men enjoy the happiness they feel.

❧

8

Becoming a Sensuous Leader

❦ What It Takes ❦

*S*eeing that you can please a man sexually and otherwise is the biggest turn on of all. Giving a little kiss with sincerity and passion can entice a man more than hours of sensuous lovemaking. Women should be more aware of the power they have over men. Any woman can be the woman that a man really wants. All it takes is how you, as a sensuous leader, can make a man feel in love, sex, and relationships. Here are some helpful hints:

1. Look for ways to improve yourself by reading, asking questions, and for getting additional training. Don't rest on what you've learned in the past. Get into the spirit of working continuously to improve your relationship with your man.
2. Be service-oriented no matter what you do for a living. Ask and help your man, don't be selfish with your talents.
3. Radiate with positive energy and avoid being negative or treating your man negatively.
4. Believe in other people by seeing good in others. Affirm your man's worth by believing in him.

5. Balance your life between your work, home, and community. Don't be too busy for your man.
6. See life as an adventure by seeing each day in a fresh, new, and exciting way. Do exciting things with your lover on a regular basis.
7. Value difference by realizing that your way is not always the right way, nor is it the only possible way. Alternatives are exciting, not a threat.
8. Take care of yourself physically through exercise. Be healthy mentally by praying or simply meditating.
9. Leave a positive impression by giving good news last. End conversations on an up note.
10. Don't gossip. Women can't afford to. Love yourself and, in turn, you will be able to love others.

Go somewhere you have never been.

9

Office Relationships

*I*f you are a career woman, the best place to find a man is through office friends or in connection with your professional surroundings. Relationships on the job are real-life relationships and very common. Being interested in someone who works with you can be either efficient or inefficient. Considering all the controversy surrounding sexual harassment in the workplace, you'd better be ready to handle the problems, trials, and tribulations that come with office relationships. Values go a long way in your professional environment and they extend further with your boss if you are always on time, efficient, and organized. Having a relationship with someone on your job might not jeopardize your competency or professionalism, but it might cause underlying problems in your life as well as that of the person you're involved with. On the other hand, if you allow your on-the-job romance to interfere with your efficiency, if you're always late, full of mistakes, and very untidy, there's a chance that you won't keep the job, even though you might have the man.

Dating someone within the same professional environment only to find out that he will be joining your company has been known to happen. Many women who held the same professional backgrounds as the men they were dating became confused, bewildered, and pressured about how to handle his joining their company. This type of on-the-job relationship by far is one of the most difficult, because the two of them have to act as if they are only professional friends. A good way to handle an office relationship is: remain professional, efficient, hardworking, and competent. Don't attract unnecessary attention by touching, holding hands, hugging or separating yourselves from the rest of the workers. Try to find other things to do at work to keep you from having lots of idle time to spend together while on the job.

When selecting clothes for the office, don't confuse evening and weekend wear with office wear. Inappropriate work attire, such as his favorite short skirt or his favorite low-cut blouse, will attract unnecessary attention from your colleagues. Be familiar with career dress codes even though you are trying to dress to please the man you love.

If you're having an intimate relationship with a man on the job and you've been promoted to his boss, be prepared for long-term exercise. It is going to take personal strength, courage, imagination, and responsible actions on your part. Sometimes your emotions will get the best of you but you'll have to push on in the face of difficult times. Sometimes it may seem impossible to handle the job and your lover, but you must strive to maintain the highest standards, looking after the smallest detail and going the extra mile by doing your very best in everything in every way. He'll have to see you in a different way than he normally does when on the job. He'll have to adjust his view to see a woman who is not only his lover but a professional person whose leadership abilities merit respect and understanding.

Try not to tie up his time at the workplace with your personal concerns and ask him to give you the same respect. These types of concerns should be saved for discussion away from the workplace. This will also allow him the opportunity to help you separate the two worlds.

When you conduct yourself in an appropriate and professional manner you will be able to handle an office relationship with a past or present lover with dignity. Don't be afraid to ask your lover to perform job-related duties when it is necessary, and most of all, ask for help without doing it in a belittling way. Don't let your position or authority get the better of you.

When away from the office, unless it is absolutely necessary, don't talk about work or the office, because then you'll be in the boss role and you'll lose all the personal attention you missed while at work. Here you can rehearse the possibilities of improving the personal side of your relationship. Map out plans and visualize overcoming any obstacles that come your way. Once you've clearly developed a workable relationship that is conducive for you and your lover you must never allow it to surface at the workplace, no matter how hot and passionate you both feel. You must remain completely professional at work. This could work in your favor because the fact that you won't be able to touch each other will turn you on even more. You don't want the affair to become idle office gossip or a company scandal. Don't cause reasons that will merit your relationship ending or one of you getting fired.

Don't get so weak for him that you forget where you are. Don't stare endlessly at him or at parts of his body while at work. If he insists, give him a tiny kiss and leave it at that, and only if no one is around. If he's previously ended a relationship and the ex-girlfriend calls, remain professional at all costs; resist eye rolling and negative responses. Remember that when you decided to have an office relationship, whether planned or not, you also chose to give up some of the freedom of expressing your affection openly. Don't allow or tolerate an attitude that will create bad feelings among each of you.

If all the men at your job are married or too old-fashioned for you, look elsewhere. Don't waste precious time toying with men who don't interest you.

The most important secret for a woman to keep is her opinion of herself.

10

Single Women

*I*n the last half of this wonderful century, women's attitudes toward being single have changed tremendously. Many opportunities are now available for single women that allows them to lead complete lives with the knowledge to overcome all obstacles. In spite of the new attitudes toward single women, nothing can change the initial shock when one loses a spouse or a lover through death or rejection. One's ego, always fragile, may be battered, and it can be a time when self-pity flourishes to the detriment of one's energies.

The goal of most women is to be happy. This is even more true for the single woman than for anyone else. Being a single woman should be looked upon as an opportunity for positive action and a time for special fulfillments. Hobbies and interests that have been dormant for years can be nurtured anew. Furthering your education can open doors to new experiences and new interests can be pursued, perfected, and enjoyed.

Being single is a time to feel proud of oneself, a time to get one's act together. It's a time to get well organized, have an affirmative attitude, and keep the eyes wide open so that one does not miss the new directions and opportunities that lie ahead.

Single women have a responsibility to society for their actions. There are times when you will be tempted to get involved with more than one man or even with a married man. You will worry about whether he is right or wrong for you. Everything that a single girl wants is not always what she needs, and every man she wants is not always right for her either.

❦ Single Woman's Ethics

Developing ethics is very important in this day and age. My single friends have given me a set of rules that they follow:

1. Keep your hands, body, lips, and mouth off your sister's or your best friend's man.
2. Don't let any man touch you or make love to you whom you don't like and don't really want to have a relationship with.
3. Give yourself completely to the man you love.
4. Respect the man you love and demand respect from him.
5. Don't tease or lead a man on, or give physical or emotional promises.
6. Keep the fidelity promised to one man; keep your word and stick to it.
7. Don't have sex with more men than you can physically handle.
8. Flirt all you want quietly; it not only builds your ego it also keeps you in practice.
9. Don't make flirtatious promises that you can't keep.
10. Be sexually responsive to your man.

Once you've become sensuous you will be an adored, admired, and attractive woman to all men, but this does not give you permission to use this gift in a hurtful way. Arrive at a set of personal ethics that are morally workable. Let these ethics remain clear in your mind and do not become a heart breaker. You want to be thought of as delicious, sensuous, sexy, and an adoring *woman*, not a user. Unpleasant situations usually accompany a person who has no sexual ethics. Take responsibility for your personal actions and your personal decisions will be easier to reach.

I believe that if you use sex as a means of making money, you will lose your sensitive edge because it then becomes a business-only attitude. But I also believe that a woman must do what she has to do to survive ... and I know that a woman of imagination will never be without money if she uses her tools in the correct way.

✱ *Single Women Affirmatives*

1. Get a job and keep it. For some women this is the most important option of all; proper preparation should begin at once. If you don't have a job, this can be one of the most difficult things you'll ever do. A single woman with a job is more positive and confident.
2. Increase volunteer work as a single woman. This helps to etch your name into this world's history.
3. Travel to new places rather than the same old place. You add more excitement and a more exploring attitude.
4. Further your education by taking some courses you've always wanted to take but never got the chance to. It's always best to increase your knowledge of the arts. This provides opportunities to meet new people. In addition, it provides networking opportunities to meet businesspeople who might be able to offer advancements to your career.
5. Follow an intensive physical improvement plan, which should involve your diet, exercise, and looks, a new hairdo or make-over, and so on.
6. Get involved in politics by joining a local political club and become active in your community's upkeep.
7. Read more often and keep yourself better informed so that your conversation has an added sparkle.
8. Seek psychological counseling if you need it. Don't be ashamed to get it all together. Shop around for the right person who will understand your personal needs.
9. Become an expert in something, whether it's dancing, jogging, or playing dominoes.
10. Make new friends of both sexes; with all the new ideas and facets of your life people will naturally want to be around you.
11. Rediscover your hidden talents in the performing and creative arts.

12. Fix up your home environment. If your home is badly in need of repairs or redecoration and you just can't afford it, then rearrange your furniture—it will give your place a new, refreshing look.
13. Entertain: Do it well, often, and with imagination. If you can't afford to buy the needed items, do as I do: invite people who don't mind pitching in and bringing the necessary things.
14. Have a pet of your choice. A pet will provide the company you need at all times and it will break the stillness of the home. And pets can also help you to become a more lovable person.
15. Remember to go to church. It's a great healer of loneliness. While in church you are a part of the greatest coming together there is, *love.*

You can either be an admirable single woman or a crusty old maid. The choice is yours.

※

Men, even if you think you understand them . . .
never let them know.

※

11

Married Women

*T*he truth is that marriages usually start with the romance that's made in heaven, but real love, like Real Women, often begins long after passion has cooled and fantasies have ended.

Let's say you're in a relationship, you feel good about yourself with this wonderful man. You see a new you, you feel good about talking to him, and you like all the things that the two of you have in common. You're having fun, you feel the fire when you are with him, and you enjoy the love and intimacy you experience with him. Just the two of you is all that's needed and you feel that you are in the middle of one of your favorite love songs.

If what I described sounds good to you, then that's the type of relationship you need to be in. But guess what usually destroys this beautiful scenario: *marriage*. This type of relationship, left on its own, will eventually die of natural causes. That's what it's supposed to do—or so some people think. Making a marriage out of it will put it on the disabled list for a lifetime. You almost have it all; a gratifying relationship, a comfortable home, a great car, and money in the bank adds to this bliss.

After the romance, marriage is the path to creation, and in between is the crossroads. As long as you can keep the stars bright, dreams flourishing, love beaming, and life hopeful, your marriage can and will survive.

There is no one answer to a successful marriage because at some point and time all couples have arguments or disagreements, and these arguments or disagreements can sometimes get out of hand, thereby creating friction that can sometimes be unrepaired. It takes lots of hard work, determination, and dedication to remain steadfast in a marriage. When living together in matrimony, whether holy or not, times can be rough if couples aren't willing to bend a little. Marriage is a give and take with many ups and downs. Each will have to give a little. Those who enter into marriage should be really in love for the duration of it, because without true love, marriage is only a relationship destined to be shortened. Marriage is a journey of self-discovery. You help to discover each other and others help to discover you. People usually chart their lives by getting married, add to the foundation by having children, and allow history to be made by doing something positive in their lifetime together.

✺ Sensuality After Marriage

Showing married women how to hold on to the creative energy and their sensuality is only part of the scope in this section. Most married women are not particularly unhappy in their marriages, nor are they taking their marriage vows lightly. Married women are seeking continuous excitement in their relationships from their husbands. Sometimes, however, they find themselves in unexpected affairs that are difficult to leave because of the much needed excitement and romance. Most women who have ventured into affairs tell me that they don't feel guilt, conflict, or remorse. Dalma Heyn, the author of *Erotic Silence of the American Wife*, which gives great reports on the wife and her erotic ventures, states that women felt awakened and revived from the emotional numbness that had settled on them after marriage once an affair begins. Many of the married women I interviewed noted that they didn't even realize the height of their sexuality until they had an extramarital affair. They also didn't realize that they had misplaced their passion until a secret friendship with a dazzling man brought them to their sexual senses. They all agreed that their affair was needed to fill a sexual, physical, financial, or emotional void. Most women who have affairs feel that their marriages improve because their tolerance levels improve. Things about their husbands that normally upset them had ceased to upset them because of their outside relationships and activities.

The desire to be sensuous had come back anew, alive, and vibrantly fresh. Since their marriages had lost the excitement, their outside relationships filled a major void. Being married has made many women feel less sexy and romantic. Their capacity for desire and pleasure in the bed was lost with their husbands. And wives aren't the only ones feeling half dead, muted, stifled, frozen, and hollow; the husbands feel that way too. These feelings are giving those once healthy marriages a bad name. Women who are married are sometimes experiencing erotic silence, which is often associated with depression in housewives. Statistics show that a higher percentage of married women are suffering from depression than single women. Marriage is proving to be more and more harmful to many women. For centuries, marriage has asked women to become selfless. It began with the woman dropping her birth name to take her husband's name on a borrowed basis. I even have women tell me that when they divorced, some of the husbands, as a part of the divorce agreement, wanted their last names back. She gives up her right to carry her name simply to justify his ownership. A woman gives up her heritage in this respect.

Many women have learned to hide their emotions from their husbands so as not to upset them. With a lover, a woman does whatever she feels at the moment, and that's what brings them closer. Her husband, she feels, gets the better her, the easier her. This is where her female sexuality as a wife dies but as a woman sometimes begins. Many married women believe that staying alive in marriage isn't just about the sex, it's about having the freedom to be yourself sexually, without the stereotyped cultural requirements. Marriage is a welcoming of the so-called good woman, one who takes care of everyone even if that means neglecting herself, which in turn means neglecting sexual gratification and satisfaction.

Today, more married women than ever before have had sex before marriage. They have several lovers, and several careers, while married. The fact that women are seeking self-fulfillment is causing many men to consider women selfish and uncaring. Many married women are incapacitated by the guilt that they cannot be the perfect wife, mother, homemaker, and wage earner. The prehistoric ideals of what it takes to qualify women as good wives are long gone. One of the reasons for this is that it's hard to live up to it and still remain healthy.

As women try to hide their past or disregard their sexual histories and pains, they suddenly begin to feel ashamed. Married women are finding it healthy to admit to their husbands their sexual wants, needs, and desires. The problem comes when he asks questions about her sexual past. She will sometimes feel ashamed, causing her true sexual self to go into hiding.

All the rituals of becoming a new and better person are significant to many women. These rituals are about cleansing and purifying. The symbolic white wedding dress represents purity, innocence, and honesty. Trying to symbolize your innocence by being perfect is not healthy. After all, no one is perfect, not even the man you love or the one you will love. This is not a perfect world.

Some women go as far as to try to hide their sexuality by diminishing the experiences that led to their sexual knowledge. Today, women are increasingly entering their marriages having had numerous sexual liaisons. Why some women are pretending that they have no sexual history is still a mystery. The "still a virgin" characteristic exists in women in order to protect their husband's ego and their reputations. Some women think that it's too bold or too unattractive to say otherwise.

Some of the phrases used to control or silence a woman in order to protect her husband's sense of manliness and sexual prowess are:

- He might disapprove.
- He might withhold sex.
- He might lose his erection.
- He might think she's selfish.
- He might call her overbearing.
- He might call her a loose woman.

A woman's expectations of sex have been so limited in the past that she sometimes gets a headache worrying about it. It's not that she doesn't get sex: she doesn't get good sex. Some women stated that, after being married for a while, pleasure dies and so does their interest in all the marital bliss that thrilled them before the marriage. Since sex is a natural expectation of marriage, when problems arise, sex usually suffers first.

Listed in chapter 18 are ways to get the marital home fires burning again. These warm to hot techniques are great for all couples who want to revive the sensuous aspects of their relationships.

❦ *Why Married Women Have Affairs*

Women who are having affairs report several reasons for their actions. One is that the communication between her and her husband is limited, sometimes even nonexistent. I am not telling women to have affairs, but I will tell women who are married, "Why not try to have an affair with your husband." In order to get your sexuality back (and if your relationship has any hope of surviving), you must begin anew with sensuality. I'm not advocating affairs, but you have to wonder what makes a woman get to this point. An affair is complicated, and its complications can easily turn a marriage into a divorce. Second, pleasure is lacking and often missing from long-time marriages. Women are not afraid to say that they need pleasure. And what they feel in an affair is passion. The third reason women are having affairs is that an affair is healing to them. It makes them feel free to make choices they wouldn't otherwise make. A woman feels free to be herself, and in turn she begins to love herself again. She also finds her lost sexual self. The last reason is she's glad to find someone with whom she can be her honest and true self. An affair allows her to share her secrets with someone who won't judge or put her down.

Affairs have been noted as being truthful; as difficult as this may seem, affairs derive from being able to express oneself openly. In an affair, a woman can be herself. She's not afraid to be honest with her lover, and that releases some of the tension that is bottled up inside of her. Women felt comfortable in an affair, because they didn't experience sexual inhibitions. The women I talked with said that the only thing they regretted about having an affair is the lying. They felt ashamed about lying to their husbands, especially if the husbands hadn't done anything to hurt them. All in all, women were glad that they had affairs.

The best way to break the cycle of affairs is to stay in tune with what your husband likes sexually and tell him what you like sexually. If you feel that the sexuality in your marriage is slipping, get to know each other again. Try not to give up on your relationship. Make an effort to show your husband your real sexual self. Once he experiences the real you, not his ideal of you, you and your sexuality will cease to be at risk.

When a woman is silent sexually, she loses her sexuality. This in turn limits her pleasure, thereby poisoning her whole sexual self. Female self-sacrifice is a matter of choice based on family values and morality codes. Excluding a woman's needs leads to a dissatisfied woman. If the woman is unhappy, the family is usually unhappy. Let your family know that the pleasures of life, fulfillment, and happiness are important to you. Let them know that you have a life too. Your children should be raised to know that even though you are their mother, you have a life too. Go out and dance once in a while. Go to the movies without the children sometimes. Being married does not mean that you lose who you are as a person. Helping your children to understand that you are a pleasure-loving individual will help them to accept women as people who are caring and fulfilled.

❧❧

Never criticize someone in front of others.

❧❧

12

Taking Care of You

❧ You've Got the Power ❧

*T*he business of taking care of you is in the hands of you more than anyone else. You've got the power to be the best that you can be if you start with a little positive personal adjustment. The first step is to turn your dream into a clearly defined goal. This may not be as impossible as it sounds. Our choices are often influenced by the values and expectations of others, which, however well intended, may not be the right choice for us. Our heart's desire may be different from what others expect of us. To find out what you really want in a man, take some private time to jot down your ideas; this will in turn force you to see things clearer. What would you truly like to have? Can the man you have or the one you are looking for help you to attain your goals? Write down all your dreams, even if at first they sound unattainable or ridiculous.

Don't be afraid to aim high and stretch yourself. If you aren't challenged by your man you may lose your enthusiasm. Practice aiming high, because you'll probably accomplish more than if you lower your expectations to make them realistic. Yet very unrealistic expectations can be a form of self-sabotage. Don't expect to find your knight in shining armor in a day or even a week—it may take longer—just remember to stick to your list of requirements for your dream boat.

Your wish list will probably have enough on it to fill a lifetime. You must narrow it down to what matters most to you, what really excites you. Look for these qualities in the man of your dreams and go after him. To help set your priorities, write down the things that you like in a man and the things that most men have said they like in you, then compare the two. You might find there is room for improvement in you.

Don't be afraid to accept the fact that you have flaws. Be a woman about it and accept your shortcomings by working to improve yourself. And don't expect the man of your dreams to be flawless, because no one is perfect, not even you.

✿ Self-assessment

Many of us take our greatest abilities so much for granted that we don't even know we have them. To bring your personal assets into focus, take inventory. On a piece of paper, list your good points and don't be modest. Divide another piece of paper into two columns. On the left, list everything special or unusual you've done—starting with your childhood, if you can remember (at least try). On the right, note the traits that these reflect. Now, compare these columns with your first sheet. You're almost certain to spot assets you didn't know you had. Last but not least, an ideal goal to catch the man of your dreams includes a plan to strengthen your personal weaknesses. Strengthening your personal weaknesses can be beneficial to meeting the man of your dreams. It will not only improve you as a person, but it will also help to improve your standards and thereby help you to reach higher goals—like finding that lucky someone who has been waiting for you all his life.

✿ Stay Flexible

Don't underestimate your ability to improve yourself no matter how many times you've already tried. If you really want to change yourself for the better, begin now. Don't put it off another day. *Do it for you!* By mapping out a plan and being flexible as well as resourceful, your dream will become a reality. Don't be so strict with yourself, loosen up and go with the flow. It is equally important to be aware of what you don't want in a man. Remember that you are becoming a confident and sensual woman, which means that you don't have to settle for a man and/or a behavior that you don't care for.

CAUTION: Being too strict in the bedroom can lead *him* to affairs.

Take long bubble baths.

13

Making Time for You

✥ Solitude ✥

*S*tudies show that women are seeking ways to relax. Guess what? One of the best ways to relax is to spend time alone. Getting away from the human race can be personally stimulating and rewarding.

Many women have found time to escape without losing compassion for their families. Solitude has rich possibilities for inner peace and personal development. Setting aside time to listen to yourself allows you the time to see the world around you more clearly. Even though good conversation is stimulating, remaining quiet for hours at a time also has wonderful benefits. Effectively incorporating solitude into your life helps you to relish and value life. By observing silent times when you don't speak, don't answer the telephone, don't read the newspaper, watch television, or listen to the radio, you can listen to yourself instead.

If you maintain silence for a day or a major part of the day, you will experience the phenomenon of solitude. Some of the best times to solve problems are through silent times. Asking yourself pertinent questions during silent times will give clarity, which in turn will give answers.

Silence should be programmed into the lives of women. Women tend to appreciate the input from their surroundings by drawing on their personal energy. Traditions of silence are ancient and full of spiritual enlightenment. Silence is known as the "holy uselessness," a cleansing of interfering vision. Even though the dictionary describes silence as passive, the absence of speech or noise, many philosophers consider it active and complex.

Silence is the voice of the soul. When you're talking or preparing to talk, you are deaf to songs within. A calmer mind is reflected during silence. Creativity flourishes as it provides a chance to grow from thoughts within. Silence can also free negative energies. Finding a time to experience solitude will help your thoughts, ideas, and creativity come through. Psychiatrist Anthony Storer, the author of *Solitude: A Return to the Self*, explains how a woman wrote him to tell how she escaped to her bedroom each afternoon, not because she needed sleep but because so much of her time was spent being alert to the needs of others that she needed to be alone.

Listening to yourself helps you to realize how much you really do or don't know. It helps to reduce the expenditure of excessive energy. Intimate silence can bring peak moments to your life.

❧ Valuable Uses of Silence

Some other valuable uses of silence are to:

- provide time for continued success
- provide opportunity to explore thoughts
- allow time for completing thoughts
- allow sensitive feelings of physical presence

Silence creates a sanctuary of self-observation. Many people distrust silence because society discourages it, therefore it is feared. Since quietness is seen as rejection or fear, it is not easy to recognize it as the inner voice of strength. Some people call it arrogance, while others see it as a form of sadness. Silence has been smothered in today's busy and noisy world of information. Reviving the values of silence are now being done at retreats and religious centers so that the mind can be nourished by tranquillity. Retreats can sometimes provide spiritual renewal. Silence releases the power to express yourself. Women are seeking contemplation in our society, and they are finding out that they don't have to leave home to obtain its benefits.

Silence can be discovered in your everyday life. Creating an environment to succeed with silent commitment is necessary to capture its true benefits. Here are some basic guidelines to follow:

1. Have the person or people with whom you live actively cooperate. Cooperation is crucial to your growth in silence. Silence can sometimes feel like rejection to your loved ones, so explain why silent times are so important to you. Using these times as curtains to enclose yourself instead of a door to shut out loved ones will help to create the support needed from your family.
2. Share your silence. Being quiet together can add new life to your relationship. It's okay to smile, to touch, and to look into each other's eyes from time to time with nonverbal communication.
3. Bring your children into your circle of silence. Encourage them to bring silent times into their own lives. It helps them to value the ability to concentrate as well as make graceful exits from arguments. It enables them to release stress by learning to calm themselves.
4. Schedule silent times. Set aside time in your day for being completely silent. You can choose the time of day as well as the amount of time you'll use. You're making time for you so you can make the rules. Remember that once you make the rules it will be easier to stick to them.
5. Explain silent times. It's your decision whether or not you explain your personal solitude. People are going to form their own opinions regardless of the true reason, so why not be unavailable during these times? After all, isn't that the purpose of silent times?
6. Ways to spend time during solitude:

   - Enjoy a long quiet ride alone in your car.
   - Take a walk in the early morning dawn.
   - Take a walk in the quiet evening dusk.

- Take a quiet walk along the beach.
- Take a silent bike ride with your lover.
- Encourage a quiet hike.
- Sit on a hilltop and recapture the essence of nature.
- Enclose yourself in your favorite room in your home and lavish solitude upon yourself.

You may want to do something different each time you reward yourself with silence. You may choose to quietly cook, clean, garden, write poems or short stories. A quiet place offers creativity. Doing nothing at all is also nice for nourishing your soul.

7. Make use of the tools available to you. When out in public, wearing headphones without playing anything keeps people from distracting you or talking to you. Use your answering machine to intercept your telephone calls while integrating silent times at home. Silence is new to many women, so exploration is different. The wonderful impact that solitude is having on my life is beneficial in the ways that I spend my days. It helps to awaken my consciousness. Solitude strengthens my senses to the natural world around me. When a bird chirps or the wind whistles I notice. I realized that I don't have to be active all the time, because I am content with being quietly me. Short sessions of solitude are appreciated because stillness is now a valuable opportunity to cherish me. I value and cherish times that I can be at peace with myself. Capturing the world of silence is an intimate relationship with oneself.

❧❧❧

Schedule quiet time for brainstorming.

❧❧❧

14

Female Maintenance

❖ Basic Hygiene ❖

*A*mericans understand the logic behind keeping the body clean and fresh. Deciding to take a bath or shower only on special days or occasions, or in an emergency, is tacky and unethical. No one wants to make love to a woman with offensive body odors. Contrary to all of the myths, hype, and commercialism, basic hygiene is not achieved only through the process of wearing clean underwear or taking a bath. It takes responsible awareness of your own personal attributes to bring out the personal bacteria-sensor in you.

❖ *Freshness*

A shower in the morning will be enough to last throughout the day. But for an after-work date, you will need higher standards of hygiene, especially if intimacy will be involved. If you practice basic feminine hygiene, even the so-called hooker's bath will adequately suffice. All that's needed is a basin to wash your vital parts. Even if lovemaking is not on your agenda, you should still take sanitary precautions before your date. Passion may develop at any time, so good grooming reflects your good hygiene to your partner—and it doesn't damage your self-esteem either.

During your monthly periods, keep tampons and sanitary napkins available. Change often to keep that fresh feeling. If you don't change often enough, odor can build up and be quite offensive and unpleasant. Bad or unpleasant odors in the love department can be quite disgusting and unfeminine. All women should see their gynecologist at least once every six months to a year, especially if they are sexually active.

At one time or another in our lives, women need protection from Mother Nature. Some women feel that herpes, body odors, bad breath, or a cold sore on the lip denotes bad grooming. This idea has not been proven to be true. Flavored douches that are supposed to save a troubled relationship often do more harm than good. A perspective that is practical, sensible, and desirable is at the very least necessary.

Feminine hygiene is presex courtesy that all women who are sexually active should adhere to. Basic hygiene makes us more enticing to the opposite sex. An investment into your feminine hygiene as a woman is worth the time, effort, and trouble.

A normal, healthy woman who bathes regularly and is conscientiously aware of basic hygiene has no need for the industrial gimmicks. Many women feel that vaginal deodorants cause rashes, are overperfumed, or diminish arousal instead of helping it. The wisdom of nature has prepared our bodies to smell clean with low maintenance and with sex comes an intoxicating aroma that should always be considered natural and wholesome. If you come across a man who would rather smell perfumes or flavored body parts before he'll acknowledge you, beware; he's interested in you for the wrong reasons.

✦ *Some Basics to Remember*

1. Prior to bathing, slough off dead skin cells with a bristle brush. This will help to bring smoothness to your skin.

2. If your skin is super dry, avoid basic bubble bath; it depletes skin of its natural oils.
3. Intensify experiences by placing candles around the tub.
4. Try to layer fragrances. Add the bath version of your favorite scent to your tub; after drying off, splash on your perfume. You'll radiate a sensuous allure.
5. Moisturize immediately after bathing. This will seal in water that skin has absorbed. Oatmeal baths are good for relaxing itchy dry skin.
6. Never soak in a very hot bath for more than twenty minutes. This could dehydrate skin. The best water temperature is 85 degrees.
7. A terrific detoxifier is a mud-bath mix.
8. Use a pumice stone on feet and a loofah on knees, elbows, and the bikini line. This will make your body feel like silk.
9. The best rule to remember is that basic hygiene should be a daily practice for all sexually active women. It's for the health of it.

※

What works for someone else may not work for you.

※

15

Personal Appearance

❦ Marketing You ❦

Remembering that you are a product to be marketed as well as packaged will help your personal appearance. You don't have to be Elizabeth Taylor or Naomi Campbell, but you'd better be attractive and have a pleasing personality. You'll never get into a man's heart, let alone his head, unless you are pleasantly attractive and appear interesting to him. Many of the ideas listed here are areas that women need to pay more attention to. If you find that you need work in these areas, begin as soon as possible to strengthen these weaknesses. Correcting these problems will start a new attitude about your appearance.

Before you can improve your appearance you must be able to recognize your faults. Don't be afraid to reevaluate yourself. The best way to do this is to answer questions about yourself that you would ask another woman. Pay close attention to those areas you personally think need extra work. If *you* think these areas need extra work then they probably do.

❀ Fashion

Collecting fashion magazines, articles, and pictures will help you coordinate and suggest ideas to improve your wardrobe. By devoting some time and effort to your appearance on a regular basis, you'll be able to find clothes that complement your finer points. Seeing a new and improved you in a short time only takes some concentrated effort.

Another way to enhance your appearance or flatter your figure is to go to department stores, boutiques, or even discount stores with a friend and try on clothing styles that you always wondered what you would look like in. Get away from your figure faults. Work with your good points. Be fashion conscious, dress for success, but don't let fashion enslave you. Be a trendsetter. If everyone else is wearing baggy pants and loose blouses, be the one to wear tight jeans and a skimpy blouse. You'll turn heads, especially men's heads. Most men are attracted to the colors a woman wears. In a survey of one hundred men, 70 percent chose blue as their favorite color, so try to wear plenty of blue. Don't buy clothes because they're practical; they tend to look cheap. And unless it jumps off the rack at you, try not to buy it. When trying on clothes, look at yourself in the mirror at all angles, sitting, standing, squatting, and bending. Observe strengths and weaknesses as you walk. Does the skirt lie smooth or slide up? Is it easy to maintain or difficult? Does your skirt hike up in the back or front? How clean do you look? Are your shoes scuffed or scarred, run over or dirty? Do your clothes appear dingy or faded? Are you wearing clothes that are too tight or too big? Don't be guilty of any of these things. If you are, start your improvements today. Be aware of your weaknesses—men certainly will.

❀ Underwear

Never, ever be caught with dirty underwear or underwear held together by safety pins. Bras held together by safety pins are one of the worst things imaginable. Invest in new bras and throw the old ones away. In the past, clean underwear was mainly suggested as an accident precaution that your parents always made sure you abided by. You took a bath whether you thought you needed it or not, and with this bath you had fulfilled the main requirement of cleanliness. Since women and sex have replaced America's favorite pastime, the care and grooming of our bodies has become a national symbol of wholesomeness. With television commercials, radio, movies, and talk-show hosts advertising flavored edible underwear, our society can't help but think basic hygiene.

And remember, very brief, thin underwear looks good on both men and women. The more sensuous, the more inviting.

❦ *Perfumes, Colognes, and Fragrances*

Unless you (or your man) have allergic reactions to perfumes, colognes, or fragrances, please wear it. Cheap imitations are simply that, "cheap" imitations. To be asked the name of the perfume you are wearing should be taken as a well-deserved compliment. If you are asked more than several times a day, it is a very good indication that you've hit on a fragrance that complements your body chemistry.

How to Wear Perfume

To get the most from your perfume, you should apply it to all the pulse spots of your body. Apply perfume and cologne to your skin, not your clothes. Chemicals in fragrances may weaken fabric or change its color.

- Don't overdo it. Your favorite cologne may clash with a roomfull of other smells, so dab lightly in various places.
- Choose a perfume or fragrance that complements your natural body odor.
- Don't mix too many different smells like deodorant, lotions, powders, perfumes. All on the same body can be quite repulsive. Many companies make lotions, body oils, perfumes,

soaps, and bath gels of the same scents. You can also find odor-less deodorants.

Where to Apply Perfumes

ankles
palms
back of your knees
bend of your elbows
behind the ears
base of the throat
bosom
inside of your wrists
between your thighs

Fragrance is seductive, and it really gets a woman noticed, but a quick spritz is not the way to go. To make a definite and lasting impression, here are some more techniques:

1. Twirl! Spray eau de toilette in the air and then spin in the mist of it all. The misty molecules of your spray should settle all over your awaiting body, hair, and clothing . . . yummy.
2. Ultimate allure! Lightly scent a cotton ball or a hankie and stuff it in your bra, pocket, or glove.
3. Re-scent! Just as you would touch up your lipstick, touch up your fragrance. This combats fade out and olfactory overload because your nose doesn't register odor once you've used it.
4. Can't afford the real thing? Less expensive bath oils and moisturizing versions are potent and *really* last! Dab on the spots mentioned above the same as you would perfume.

A Few More Tips

- Check out new eau de parfumes. These fall between toilet water and perfume in strength but are much less expensive.
- Use matching bath and body products to layer your fragrance.

- Multifloral and oriental scents stay vital the longest and are the most arousing.
- Avoid buying perfume just prior to menstruation—your sense of smell is weakest then. (The birth control pill is said to also alter odor-detecting ability.)
- Hair is a fabulous perfume vehicle. Mix a few drops with your conditioner, then run it through your hair.
- The best application time is right after you shower; your open pores will soak up the aroma.
- Dab petroleum jelly on your pulse points, and then apply perfume directly to these areas.
- Apply perfume and cologne before putting on your jewelry. The alcohol and oils in your favorite scent can cause a cloudy film on both real gold and costume jewelry.
- Don't stick to one fragrance all year long; temperatures affect the intensity of a fragrance. Use heavy scents and oils in winter but lighter fragrances in smaller quantities during the summer.

Some questions you should ask yourself:

How does wearing fragrance make you feel?
Do you wear fragrance for yourself or other people?
How often do you wear fragrances?
How many different fragrances do you own?
When do you wear your fragrance?
How often do you switch fragrances?
When was the last time you purchased a new fragrance?

❦ *Neatness Counts*

Even if you are a little on the wild side, the punk rock–type person or the mild, meek, and mannered person, you should still be neat, clean, and attractive in your appearance. No runs in your hosiery, no holes in your socks, no faded fake earrings, no running mascara, no smudges in your makeup, no smeared lipstick, no scuffed handbags, no missing buttons, no broken zippers, no dangling threads, and never wear day-old makeup. Remove old makeup on a daily basis. Remember to touch up frequently. Throw away torn or faded dresses or blouses. Use as cleaning rags only.

❧ Shoes

When wearing shoes, flats can be worn in your true size, but heels should be at least a half size larger for comfort. This method also eliminates corns and calluses, which are not a pretty sight on a woman or man. Shoes on a woman should display a sense of purity and cleanliness. With shoes you'll be wearing a lot, consider a pair made of leather or woven fabric. These materials breathe and are usually more comfortable than shoes made of synthetic materials.

Wear shoes that complement your feet. A friend might be able to wear slingbacks because of the size and shape of her foot, but you might not. Make sure your shoe wardrobe includes a pair of shoes in a neutral color that goes well with a wide range of clothing colors. Be selective, and true to yourself, as well as complimentary.

Shoes should be:

clean and shining,
neat and fitting,
not too tight or too small,
with well-kept, clean, polished, and even heels,
and with well-kept and unscuffed toes.

Having Heel Appeal

Women have their own interpretation of heels. They think of heels as their stature, pedestals, and they wear them as a sensual statement. High heels entice some men because of the sexuality they reveal. Heel appeal gives legs curves and elegance. Women with long legs can create dramatic effects when they don a pair of high heels. High heels give added height to a woman's frame.

❧ Nails

Keep your fingernails and toenails well manicured and polished, even if it's only a coat of clear polish. Be sure to make it a habit to keep under nails as clean as possible. Beautiful nails are a plus. Don't forget to polish your toenails also. Remember to wear nail polish that complements your natural skin tone. Wearing the same color as your best friend may not be the best choice for you. What looks good on her may not compliment you. Remain an individual by wearing what looks good on you.

Caring for Your Hands and Nails

1. When nails chip excessively, it may be caused by the nail polish remover you're using. Leave your nails unpainted for a few days to see if the condition improves.
2. When you're preparing anything with lemon and vegetable juices, which contain acids that are hard on fingernails, rinse your hands often under cool running water.
3. To break the habit of nail biting or cuticle chewing, carry a tube of cuticle cream with you. Whenever you start to nibble, put the cream on your cuticles instead. You'll promote healthy nails and break yourself of a bad habit.
4. To prevent nail polish from thickening, store it in the refrigerator.
5. To rescue nail polish that has become hardened or gummy, place the bottle in a pan of boiling water for a few seconds to get the polish flowing smoothly again.
6. A light color nail polish gives your hands the illusion of being longer and more graceful.
7. Use a diamond-dust nail file or an emery board. File nails in one direction only.
8. To prevent nail polish bottle tops from sticking, rub the inside of the cap and the neck of the bottle with a thin layer of petroleum jelly.

❀ Hair

Designer clothing, perfectly applied makeup, and fine jewelry are all wasted if your hair looks greasy, dull, or messy. Fortunately, no one needs an expensive professional hair salon or expensive hair products to have hair that looks professionally cared for and styled. With the right techniques for shampooing, drying, and styling your hair, it can be one of your most attractive features.

Invest in a good haircut and hair style that compliments the beautiful features of your face. Every hair style is not intended to be worn by every face. Be different, yet complimentary. The basic cut is the key to an attractive hair style. If the cut is not right, no matter what you do, the style will not last; it will not flatter your face, nor will it look fresh and neat on a daily basis.

Unless you are a part of a leper colony, underarms and legs should be sheared of any hair. And try not to wear that mustache that keeps peeking out. Have electrolysis if needed. Pubic hair can be trimmed to help keep unwanted odors to a minimum. Be sure to trim or shave any long hairs that peek out from your panties and bikinis. It's unattractive and barbaric to present yourself with hairs hanging out of your underwear.

As far as the rest of your body hair, it's up to you whether you trim or shave it. Don't get carried away with trying to remove any hair other than from the underarms and legs, or obvious pubic hairs. The hair surrounding your navel or your nipples is not what we call unwanted hair. Once you begin to shave hair from these places it will come back in triplicate. Whatever hair you decide is unsightly, be consistent in removing it regularly. Women tend to become very relaxed about such things when they are involved in a long-term relationship. This is being personally inconsiderate. The abrasive stubble can ruin a once beautiful situation.

If you have dandruff, use a good dandruff shampoo. Try the following treatment every two weeks: Section your hair and rub your scalp with a cotton pad saturated with plain rubbing alcohol. Let the alcohol dry, then brush your hair and rinse thoroughly with warm water, but don't shampoo.

You can check with your local pharmacist on which product or brand is best to use for your type of hair. After shampooing, rinse your hair with cool water to seal moisture in the hair shafts.

Other things you should know about hair care:

- To distribute the natural oils in your hair, bend over and brush your scalp and hair from back to front until the scalp tingles; then massage your scalp with your fingertips.

- To cut down on static electricity, dampen your hairbrush before brushing hair. Avoid using a brush on wet hair, because it is subject to breakage.
- To get a fuller look to your hair style, bend over so that your hair falls forward and blow the underneath layers dry first.
- To perk up curly, permed hair between shampoos, lightly mist your hair with fresh water and push the curls into place with your fingers.
- Dull, lifeless hair can be a sign of a poor diet. Try cutting down on cholesterol and fats.
- Wait at least forty-eight hours after coloring hair before shampooing it. Every time you wet hair, you open the cuticle, so give hair time to seal in the color.
- Hair sprays, mousses, gels, and other styling aids build up over time despite judicious shampooing and rinsing. If you find this happening, buy a clarifier, which removes product buildup without stripping essential oils. Make your own by mixing one (1) part vinegar with twenty (20) parts water.

✺ *Eyes*

Eyes are the windows to the soul. They tell the world who you are. Some techniques used to add allure and make eyes ravishing:

1. Apply regular foundation over the entire lid area. This helps everything else adhere.
2. Pluck your eyebrows from underneath, then fill in with eye shadow that's a shade lighter than your natural color. Some women draw on the shape they want before they pluck or after they pluck.
3. Use mascara on your lashes. Then, if you need more depth or thickness, paste one or two rows of false lashes on top.
4. Warm a spoon slightly with a cigarette lighter, then curl real or fake lashes over the spoon to bead and blend (professional model's secret).
5. Gently pull your skin around your eyes outward as you sweep back liquid liner across your upper lid line.

6. Define the bottom of your eyes with brown eye pencil, both underneath and inside them.
7. Dot concealer one tone lighter than your skin over dark circles that usually surround the eyes. Smooth in to blend.
8. Use two shades of eyebrow pencil to make your brow color look more natural.

More Ways to Make Eyes Ravishing

- Use your eyes as a flirtatious vehicle to send signs, signals, and gestures in positive ways.
- Healthy habits such as placing sliced raw potatoes over and under eye bags for ten minutes can help your assets. The chemical composition draws the excess water from the skin that causes puffiness.
- A Hawaiian trick for thicker lashes: apply a bit of castor oil with fingers before bed. This encourages new growth.
- Plucking is a must! Try icing before you pluck to ease pain.
- You can use an ordinary number 2 pencil to fill in brows.
- Revive tired eyes by covering with cucumbers, or kiwi slices (leave on for ten minutes).
- Try subtle-colored contact lenses for a change in eye color.
- Invest in good makeup brushes. This will help you to apply foolproof makeup.
- To make the whites of your eyes appear whiter, line your lower lashes with a deep-blue color stick.
- To bring out deep-set eyes, apply a light, frosted shadow on both your lids and brow bone, using a darker shade in the eyelid crease.
- Avoid matching the color of your eye shadow to the exact shade of your eyes. The colors will cancel each other out, making your eyes look drab.
- Protect your eyelashes with a thin coat of waterproof mascara whenever you're outdoors.
- For thick-looking lashes, apply mascara and let it set for a few minutes. Then add a little more mascara to the tips. If you use an eyelash curler, curl the lashes before you add mascara to the tips.

- Applying fresh mascara over the old will make your lashes brittle. Be sure to use mascara remover to clean your lashes before going to bed.
- When your mascara begins to dry out, run hot water over the tube for a few minutes to soften the remaining mascara inside.
- Limit the use of eye drops during the summer—overuse can be harmful.
- Small eyes can be made to look larger by applying eye shadow under your lower lashes starting at the center of the eye and blending to the outer corner. Sweep the color along the brow bone out to the side of your eye.

The spirit behind your eyes is only one of the many keys to unlocking sensuality. Using your eyes as a creative and seductive tool can produce some of the most pleasurable moments to remember.

❦ *Skin*

Your skin is the indicator of your overall health. If you're not healthy, it will be reflected in your complexion. But that doesn't mean you should neglect your skin if you're feeling fine.

Some easy ways to clear up your skin problems:

1. Don't play with it; put notes on mirrors to remind yourself not to pick it.
2. Try not to touch or lean your cheek on the cradle of the phone; particles of food or secretions from the mouth may be there.
3. To flush out impurities, drink lots of water.
4. Never go to bed before removing makeup. If you hate to sleep with a naked face, dust lightly with pressed powder and blush.
5. Get at least eight hours of sleep per night.
6. Use oil-free powder during exercise if you must wear makeup so that your pores won't clog. Clean your face with astringent after your workout.
7. To diffuse stress, take vitamin C.

8. Avoid laundry detergents with sodium laurylsulfite (pimple-producing ingredient).
9. Take ibuprofen when cystlike pimples appear. This also reduces the inflammation.
10. To calm facial redness, take ice breaks twice a day for two minutes. Place cold towels or towels with crushed ice gently against the face for several minutes each morning. You'll feel revitalized as well as fresh and perky.
11. Switch to low-dose or triphasol birth control pills.
12. Be sure to read all cosmetic labels. Avoid products containing isopropyl myristate, isopropyl palmitate, stearic acid, decyloleate, mineral oil, lanolin, and fragrance.
13. Avoid getting hair styling products on your forehead.
14. Use makeup that camouflages. Apply oil-free foundation with cover cream; with a tiny makeup brush, dab away imperfections. Last, pat lightly with translucent powder to set.
15. A surprising blemish fighter is *sex*.
16. Don't worship the sun. It's a myth that the sun dries zits. It actually damages follicles, which makes the outbreak worse. Women of all colors should use sunblocks that contain titanium dioxide or oil-free ones.
17. Do not apply perfumes, fragrances, or colognes to your face—they can have irritating effects.
18. If you drive a convertible, be sure to apply sunblock on hot summer days.
19. Make it a habit to always wear a moisturized sunscreen when out of doors, both winter and summer. The sun's rays can burn you even if the air feels cool, and sunlight reflected off water or the whiteness of snow can be particularly powerful.
20. No matter what your skin type is, use a high-protection lotion the first time you are in the sun and don't expose your skin for more than fifteen minutes. Use a total sunscreen on your face and the back of your hands, because these are constantly exposed to the sun's rays.
21. If you usually wear makeup, give your skin a chance to breathe one day a week by going without.
22. During the winter, use a humidifier to lessen the drying effects indoor heat has on your skin.
23. Take baths in the evening to avoid exposing your skin immediately to the outdoor air.

Special Note

Even darker skin complexions can get skin cancer; don't exempt yourself from sunblock because of your race.

❧ *Lips*

- Always protect your lips with a thin coating of colorless lip balm whenever you aren't wearing lip gloss or lip color.
- For a long-lasting lipstick, apply a generous coat, then let it set for about two minutes. Blot with a tissue, puff on some powder, and then apply another generous coat of lipstick. Wait again and blot.
- Choose warm, tawny lip colors for office light.
- To make full lips appear slimmer, draw a lip line inside your natural lip line and fill with a darker shade of lip color.
- To make thin lips appear fuller, draw a lip line outside your natural lip line and fill with a lighter shade of lipstick.
- If your upper and lower lips are uneven, apply makeup foundation over your lips, then fashion a new lip line with a pencil a shade darker than your lip color.

❧ *Foundation and Blush*

- Test the color of foundation by applying a drop to your face or neck rather than the back of your hand. If possible, check the color in natural light by a door or window rather than under fluorescent lights in the store.
- In the winter, use oil-based, rather than water-based, makeup to protect your skin against dry, cold air.
- In the summer, switch to a water-based foundation to help moisturize your skin, but use waterproof makeup for lips, eyes, and lashes to prevent running and smearing in the heat.
- To apply foundation evenly, use a damp sea sponge, which allows the color to blend evenly and gives the most natural-looking coverage.

- To emphasize facial contours, select a foundation that's a shade lighter than your tan.
- Use a large makeup brush to dust translucent powder lightly over your face after you've applied makeup Then further set the makeup with a light spray of mineral or ordinary water.
- To help your foundation last longer and give better coverage, mix it with an equal amount of skin freshener.
- To help camouflage a double chin, apply blush under the chin, then blend it upward to the bone and across toward the outer edges of the jaw.

Happiness is a do-it-yourself project.

16

Body Balance

❖ Diet and Toning ❖

Most women believe that their attitudes about food are in constant conflict with their desire to be slimmer. Trying to balance a quality exercise program in this hectic society can create roadblocks for women who work, cook, clean, and nurture their families around the clock. Balancing an exercise program has a multitude of benefits for women of all ages. To be at your best physically, mentally, and emotionally as well as sexually, women must start by getting a complete physical evaluation. Working out with aerobics on a constant basis will help to increase your stamina and add strength. However, aerobic exercise alone does not provide a balanced fitness program. If you expect your lover to like what he sees, then you need to get off your fanny waiting on a miracle to come to you. As you work out with aerobics and begin to slim down, strength training will enable you to preserve lean body mass.

Getting plenty of exercise will help your glands work toward being in tip-top shape. The major cause of weight problems lies within the foods women tend to eat. Problems can come from your lifestyle, professional life, daily scheduled eating time, and your intake of food. None of us can ignore food easily. Start paying closer attention to what you put in your body and you will begin to lose weight in a healthy way. You will notice that the weight will stay off and not resurface after a few months.

Most people don't realize that they don't have to diet, they just need to reduce their intake of certain foods. Eliminating that extra slice of pie or that ice cream cone before bed can reduce your fat cell increase.

⊕ Nutrition

Keep a food diary for one week (seven days). Write down everything that you put into your mouth. *Everything!* Even the cigarettes that you smoke should be entered into your weekly diary. Include snacks no matter how small. If you chew a piece of bubble gum write it down. It will be a little uncomfortable at first, but keeping an accurate record will only help you to become the woman that you want to be with the body that you so deserve. Have a dietitian evaluate your diary at the end of the week (don't be shy or embarrassed). A dietitian will be able to tell you which foods are high in fat content or if your portions are too much for your body to burn off effectively. Eating out can often be the source of too many wrong foods. Cook a special meal for your man at home. He'll enjoy the treat. Since you'll be watching your intake you'll be more careful of what you eat.

Restaurant foods often contain hidden fats and oils and portions are usually larger than those prepared at home. Remember that larger portions make larger bodies. Plan your menu and calorie intake and then stick to it. By having to plan your meals ahead of time, they will be balanced and nutritional and you will get the most food for your calories.

⊕ Eating Plan

Some nutritionists and dietitians feel that your eating plan should initially start with 1,200 calories daily. After feeling dizzy and suffering headaches for a day, I realized that my calorie intake was too low. Experimenting with different calorie amounts will allow you to see how many calories you should eat in order to lose weight or maintain your present weight, or even to gain weight.

Each person's metabolism is different, and each individual needs to monitor her own body to see how many calories can be consumed. Becoming a conscientious woman will be your goal. Here is the most basic formula to use when trying to figure out how many calories you can eat and still lose the weight that you desire to lose. If you want to gain weight, add calories to what you are already consuming and your job will be easier.

- Estimate the number of calories needed per day for weight maintenance (based on sedentary lifestyle) by multiplying your weight in pounds by 10. Example: $140 \times 10 = 1,400$.
- For a safe weight loss of approximately one pound per week, subtract 250. Example: $1,400 - 250 = 1,150$.

If you exercise, make sure to factor in the number of calories you burn during your workout. You will only have to cut 50 calories out of your diet, rather than 250, in order to lose a half pound per week.

Read the labels on everything you eat. You might still be able to eat your favorite foods if you just monitor what you eat on a regular daily basis. (Avocados and nuts, which I love, have a high percentage of fats.) Watch out for sugar-free products; this *only* means that they are free of sucrose but not free of the many other types of sweeteners that are no better for you nutritionally (honey, corn syrup). Look for foods that are enriched, fortified, low-sodium, or have added fiber.

In products with nutrition labels, make sure to check out the grams of fat per serving. Only 30 percent of your total caloric intake per day should come from dietary fats (for people who are trying to lose weight, their daily intake should be less). If you consume 1,200 calories a day, only 360 of those should be from fat.

There is no need to give up your joy for food. Here are some tips to enjoy your meals without jeopardizing your calorie limit.

- Set a realistic limit, remembering to nutritionally balance your menu. (Don't order a salad and then top it by ordering dessert.)
- Incorporate an appetizer or bread or both into your calorie count so you're not famished by the time the meal is served.

- Before ordering an entrée, consider how it is prepared. You'll save a lot of calories if it's broiled or grilled dry with sauce on the side.
- Any leftover calories can be applied toward dessert or alcohol. Neither are forbidden; just plan for the calories that are your limit.

✹ Changing Behaviors

Some people think food represents festivity and comfort, but others turn to food when life isn't fun. Food is considered a quick fix to make people feel better. Sometimes it does so for only a short while. After indulging, people feel worse about themselves. Work on recognizing times when you're vulnerable to overeating or simply snacking out of depression or anxiety. Use alternatives like calling a friend, going for a walk, or being around other people, and don't forget the most important alternative of all:

Keep a food diary. Record your mood along with what and how much you eat. Usually, when a person is tired, too busy, or bored, the result is overeating. When you feel like snacking, eat healthy snacks. Instead of chocolates, chips, or candy, select fruits, vegetables, whole-wheat pretzels, or frozen diet desserts.

Learning to eat the correct foods is just like learning to play a musical instrument. It takes a lot of practice. You'll slip up from time to time, but the important thing is to get back in touch with your goals and never give up on improving yourself.

✹ Body Metabolism Matters

As many of us suspected, some people are born with a higher metabolism. You can boost your metabolism if you don't give up. Exercises using your leg muscles can increase your metabolism the most. Aerobics exercises like running, walking, stair climbing, and bicycling fires metabolism up. Strength training can also speed up your metabolism permanently because lean muscle tissue burns calories faster than fatty tissue. But increasing muscle mass takes months of work. Be patient; don't give up, because you'll enjoy as well as appreciate the end results.

The best weight-loss plan is to cut calories only moderately, but you must be more active. If you're less active because of laziness—but you claim it's due to age—then just get up and start moving. Force yourself. You need to be active if you're going to drop those unwanted, unhealthy pounds. Start at a beginner's pace if you haven't exercised for a long time. Then, gradually build up your endurance to do more sets as well as repetitions.

❀ *Walking to Help Metabolism*

Walking burns calories, tones muscles, strengthens bones, and only costs the price of a pair of sneakers made for walking. Walking can be taken up at any age or fitness level.

There is always something that can be said about walking. Thinking to put one foot in front of the other should sum it up, but not so. You don't even have to have sweat pouring down your face to enjoy the benefits of walking. You help your heart by walking because as you walk faster, your heart beats faster. That in turn helps to tone your heart muscle causing better efficiency in pumping blood. You will function with less fatigue and your energy level will increase. It also helps to lower your chances of acquiring heart disease when you exercise. Many people believe that walking increases your appetite, but it really doesn't. It increases your metabolism as it curbs your appetite.

❀ *Tension Relief: With Walking*

Walking also firms and strengthens your calves, thighs, ankles, feet, stomach, hips, and buttocks. The strong arm swing during walking helps you to maintain balance; proper stride will tone and strengthen your shoulders, upper back, chest, and arm muscles. Walking can also help ease your feelings of tension and anxiety. And walking has a continuous tranquilizing effect.

Be sure to stretch your muscles before walking, to avoid strain. Toward the end of your walk, gradually slow down so that your muscles have a chance to cool down. Don't go full speed and then come to a complete stop. This is not good for any part of your body.

❦ Walking in Water

To burn up to 500 calories per hour, just wade in a nearby pool, lake, or beach. You won't even have to get your hair wet during warmer months. Remember to apply sunblock. Walking in water as a part of your exercise program is great for losing those unwanted inches that you find difficult to lose.

Water helps to support you as you walk, burning calories at a brisk rate without putting undo strain on your joints. You can begin walking in water that is only knee deep and of cool temperatures. Warm water will drive the heart rate up too high, so be careful. Move backward, forward, sideways, with lengthy strides. Work a bit harder with waist-high water while trying to maintain a twenty-minute workout of walking. Walking with your arms in the water will burn even more calories and provides a more complete workout.

A good tip to remember is if you are tired of pulling and tugging as you try to put your swimsuit on, the water workout will give you more incentive to work those pounds off. At least if you exercise in the water your flab won't be seen and you can burn off inches and calories at the same time.

❦ Splash Techniques

Aqua-aerobics is the latest craze at health clubs. Just like water walking, try water jogging as a part of your aerobic workout. The advantage is that there is no stress involved in splash techniques. This is great even in as little as one foot of water. I'm presently creating a book with a workout program for water aerobics. Look for it to be released soon.

When I was younger, as a part of my gymnastics workout, my coach would have us jog in tubs of water. It worked the hell out of our legs and it increased our cardiovascular endurance levels. It was *great*.

❧ *Other Wonders of Water*

Many women know that water works wonders. Even though the statement is straightforward the message is sometimes confusing. We tend to take the benefits of water for granted. Of course we splash, swim, bathe, paddle, shower, and even drink it, but we need to check out some of the marvelous facts of our most prized natural resource.

❧ *Drink Plenty of Liquids*

Your physical being is about 70 percent water. Water helps you digest your food, and it carries the nutrients in your body. It keeps your joints lubricated and it helps to carry waste from your body. Surviving without food is possible for many weeks, but without water you wouldn't survive more than a few days. Water constantly flowing throughout your body assures your life. Water aids in keeping skin moisturized as well. As we grow older, water becomes more important. Keeping hydrated will assure comfortable body mechanisms that are sometimes slowed down with age.

❧ *Bottled Water*

Some water that has been considered filtered and chlorinated isn't as good as bottled water. There are many brands on the market and the 1.6 billion gallons of bottled water that's consumed by Americans boils down to at least eight gallons per capita. With all the varieties there are, you are sure to find one you like. If you have questions about your local reservoir, call your city's and/or county's water company.

Here's a list of the types of bottled water:

Spring water: sources are from natural underground springs
Sparkling water: has natural and added carbonation
Seltzer: filtered and sodium-free; during the bottling process it's carbonated

Club soda: filtered and carbonated; mineral salts and minerals
added for taste (has a higher sodium count)
Mineral water: ground water with minerals added; composition
varies
Bulk water: purified, distilled, deionized; calcium or magnesium
salts added for taste (sold in one gallon jugs)

❀ Wet and Watery Lettuce

A technique used in agriculture substitutes a solution of water
and chemical fertilizers for soil. Called hydroponics, it's been
around since World War II. These vegetables are bland and a little
watery, but the advantages of year-round availability is great. I've
had several women tell me that they place pieces of watery lettuce
like little patches over their eyes to reduce early morning swelling.

❧❦❧

Change is inevitable—so welcome it.

❧❦❧

17

Douching and Cleansing

❦ Cleansing the Vagina ❦

Women should be very selective as to whether they should cleanse the vagina and/or the anus. Both openings have their own special odors and body fragrances. Just as fingerprints are different, so are body odors. Every woman's body is unique and so her odors are uniquely different. No two smell the same. This odor varies for many reasons. Many things are a common factor in body odors, so before you begin to douche excessively, get in tune with your body to find out why you possess these odors.

Some common reasons for odors:

diet and eating habits
medications
exercise program
rest factor
body oils and perfumes
lotions
powders

water source
soap or cleansing product
skin type or condition of skin
bodily functions
frequency of sex
masturbation habits and fluids
vaginal secretions
menstrual cycle

Douching is not necessary to cleanse the vagina. The normal, healthy vagina naturally cleans itself. If you feel it personally necessary to douche after your period, you can do so with little worry of developing problems. Women who douche too frequently, however, can destroy the colonies of beneficial bacteria that normally inhabit the vagina, leaving it vulnerable to organisms that cause vaginitis (inflammation of the vagina). Most women douche when they smell unpleasant odors or experience excessive discharges. But the vagina will not have a continuous bad odor unless an infection exists, so if you notice an unusual smell or discharge that you can't seem to combat, rather than trying to douche it away see your doctor.

Good personal feminine hygiene makes oral sex more attractive, but you don't need to douche in preparation for oral sex. Simply wash the external vaginal area carefully. A dash of perfumes or fragrances on your inner thighs or your pantyline will add sensual allure for your partner. I recommend a perfume that's light and pleasant, not too spicy or too strong. You don't want your lover to love the smell and hate the taste because you've overdone the perfume.

❖ Cleansing the Clitoris

The clitoris is hardly ever mentioned when we talk about cleansing the sex organs, but it needs proper cleansing also. Located at the head of the vagina, covered by fluffy skin under the labia, it needs to be dealt with in more ways than one. It is often called the love button because of its sensitive nature in helping women to achieve orgasm. As you pull the skin of the labia back, take a cotton swab and with circular motions gently clean until the white mucous that is embedded there is eliminated. Don't try to clean it too well because the natural secretions of this orifice are healthy. You want to cleanse it only after lovemaking or after your monthly period. Sometimes the fluids from sex and your period hide inside the skin folds of your love button causing odors that are rarely detected. Bacteria and unwanted odors in this area are difficult to detect because we never look for them.

❦ *Cleansing the Anus*

The anus should be cleaned just as any other part of the body should be cleaned. Washed carefully to rid it of all excrement and bacteria that settle after a bowel movement. Wiping with tissue after having a bowel movement is not enough to say that it is thoroughly cleaned. Time and care should be given to cleaning it well.

With the constant streaks, skid marks, or mud marks (as women call them) showing up on a regular basis in our son's, husband's, or boyfriend's underwear, we women should begin to wonder just how clean our men are. Women have personal accessories that are included within their douche packets that can be used to clean the anus, but men are left to dig, pull, wipe and scuff endlessly only to share their skid marks with the rest of the wash. The anus should be wiped and cleaned thoroughly after each bowel movement. One of the best ways suggested by women to clean the anus is to wipe from front to back several times after a bowel movement. Cup the toilet tissue and wipe again, even if you think you've cleaned all residue, wipe one more time for practical measures. You'll use more tissue than normal, but it's worth it to feel clean. I've gone to great lengths to find the answer to an obvious but well-kept secret: Why do men have bowel streaks in their underwear on a regular basis? My theory is that the number of times men actually sit down to use the commode is far less than women. Therefore, women wipe their anus more often than men. You see, the fact is men stand while urinating, women sit, so women wipe 50 percent more often than men. Whether it is wiping their vagina or their anus, women still wipe more often.

Women are taught as children to wipe their vaginal sections after each use on the toilet. We are taught and trained to wipe from the front toward the back, which leads me to believe that we actually wipe our anus with almost every toilet use. Each woman that I interviewed said that almost every single time they used the toilet they wiped their anus whether intentionally or not. It was primarily a habit. Therefore, men are susceptible to producing longtime streaks in their underwear far more than women.

Set aside time to pamper yourself.

18

Awakening Your Sexual Senses

❦ Warm to Hot ❦

While gently teasing your man you can strike an erogenous zone. Lightly massage the inside of his arms and his palms, then gently massage the inside of his thighs as you knead them. Run your fingers over other parts of his body that you consider just as erogenous. The good thing about this type of awakening is that you can do it with your clothes on or off. You can also do these things as you snuggle in front of the television, a lit fireplace, or even when passing one another in the living room.

- While hugging him, give him a teasingly slow rotation of your pelvic bone against his groin.
- Massage the back of his neck.
- Stroke his body parts that you most like.
- Make an erotic telephone call or leave a love note for him in his lunch or briefcase.
- Take full advantage of all erections.
- Wrestle naked playfully as you catch him stepping out of the tub or shower.

- Greet him at the door naked.
- Put on some mellow music and get him away from the TV so you can dance slowly and erotically.
- Take a bath together.
- Take a shower together in a darkened room.
- Tell him that you love to look at and touch his naked body.
- Buy him a pair of satin boxers.
- Read *Will the Real Women . . . Please Stand Up!* to him as erotically as you can.
- Give each other foot massages and relaxing back rubs.
- Kiss each other passionately every time you kiss.

❧ *Phase One: Sensitivity*

Let's begin this phase by doing something very simple. To test your sensitivity, go to a secluded spot of your choice—it can be your car, your lounge, or your bed. It doesn't matter where as long as you're alone. Close your eyes and let your body go limp. Think of long hard objects only. Frozen link sausages, chicken legs, empty bottles, cucumbers, carrots, a dildo, or even a long, erect, and hard penis. I hope I've helped to awaken your senses by now.

Memorize your favorite objects: size, shape, length, width, and texture. Think of all the qualities, like the smoothness of each. Compare the differences, the likes and dislikes. You'll be amazed and sometimes excited by your memory.

For a week, practice your memory skills this way to increase your sensitive awareness of shapes, sizes, and textures. This improves your sensitivity toward your sexual partner. Another good thing that you can do is to change the items each day and discover how the objects come to life in your hands as you touch, feel, and caress them with your eyes closed. Bring out your sensitive side with each touch. Get mentally lost in the feelings of each object.

❧ *Phase Two: Awareness*

In this sexual awareness phase, you'll memorize the items in phase one that you got to know. Manipulate your mind, arouse your sexual appetite, and automatically feel the heat. If you practiced the phase one sensory tactics as suggested, you should feel a tingle or goose bumps as you think of the objects.

To help you, think of your favorite long, hard, and sensuous objects slowly sliding inside you. Imagine the depth of it all as it eases out under your control. Don't be shy or inhibited. You've got to get past the idea of it all in order to grasp the technique fully. I promise you, once you can imagine the eroticism of it, you will feel the tingle of it. To help you to coast into this pleasure center of your brain, imagine yourself gripping your lover's long, hard, erect penis between your hands, your breasts, down your stomach, and slowly sliding against your clitoris and finally inside your wet vagina. As your vagina dampens with anticipation you'll feel a tingle of pleasure. Ummmmmmm, imagine these pleasures as you tingle your way to sensuality.

❀ *Phase Three: Moisturize*

This phase is the most important one and you should do it each night before falling asleep. Run a warm bath and add your favorite bath oil, cologne, or fragrance. As the tub is filling, rub your body with your favorite moisturizer and scan your favorite book—*Will the Real Women . . . Please Stand Up!* Unwind and let your senses lock in. Play your favorite relaxing music and turn all the lights off.

Tell everyone that lives with you that you would like some privacy and relaxation. Light a small scented candle and sit in your freshly filled tub of water. Relax completely—both physically and mentally. Guide your mood and enhance your senses by thinking of nothing but relaxation and the pleasures of sensuality. Let your quiet surroundings swallow you up as the scents entice you. Let the flickering light from the candle dance in your mind as you slip into an intensely mellow mood. Allow the water to envelop your sensitive body. Let the mood romance your every desire as you humble your soul to the pleasures of it all. Pull a handful of water toward you and feel the water as it trickles down your chest, between your breast, and across your neck. Close your eyes now and listen to your soft music as you gather in all the peacefulness around you. Feel the water as it surrounds your entire body. Discover the smoothness of the water as it ripples to your every movement.

Grasp mental pictures of the water and your body sitting in it. Lose yourself in your thoughts, and when you begin to feel drowsy, remove your new self from the tub. Included in the next section are sensuous beauty baths that will enable you to become a more seductive woman.

✱ Phase Four: Enjoying You

Each person's body is unique. In this phase of sensuality, you will be able to enjoy your own body. This enables you to reach maximum pleasures in lovemaking. No matter what size your body is, you are special. Take time to discover you. Have pride in yourself as well as your body. Take your towel and dry off very slowly. With every stroke of your towel blot yourself gently as if you are drying off a newborn baby's bottom. Apply your favorite body lotion to your entire body. To help improve your senses, rub your favorite lotion on your body with your eyes closed. Try to get to know your body as you incorporate this sensuality phase. Know where every hump, bump, and mole is on your body. Begin a whole new friendship with your body. After all, you are getting to know you.

Once you've blotted off any remaining lotion, pull your bedcovers back and ease into your bed naked. Sensuously sexy is how you should feel. You should fall asleep almost instantly. Sweet dreams. Don't forget to blow out any remaining candles before preparing for a good night's sleep.

✱ Phase Five: Sensuous Baths

Phase five consists of several types of beauty baths that can be used as a sensual stimulation toward other fulfilling moments. Your mind, body, and love life will all benefit from these baths.

1. APHRODISIAC

Turn your tub into foreplay, invite him to join you in a bath spiked with two to three tablespoons of grated gingerroot, fresh mint leaves, and cinnamon. For an added arousing effect, feast on champagne and your favorite appetizers.

2. Sleep Inducer

Soak in tea instead of drinking it before going to bed. Steep four bags each of tangerine lavender and chamomile tea in a pot of boiling water. Add this mixture to your bath and submerge yourself in the tub. Close the room up to seal in the steamed aroma. Relax for ten minutes or more as you inhale the scents. You'll be able to fall asleep sooner after the sleep-inducer bath.

3. At Home Salt Glow

Prepare a grainy mixture of two cups of Epsom salt and one cup of baby oil. Set the mixture aside as you soak in plain warm water for ten to fifteen minutes, then stand up and rub the concoction into your legs, arms, belly, back, and buttocks. Rinse in the shower, dry off, and smooth on more baby oil.

4. After Sports Muscle Relaxer

After a good workout to ease muscle spasms or tightness, spice warm tub with a teaspoon of dry mustard, thyme, and lavender. Soak for ten to fifteen minutes. Don't forget to:

- soak no longer than twenty minutes, to prevent dehydrating
- best water temperature is 85 degrees
- use a pumice stone on feet and a loafah on knees, elbows, bikini line—you'll feel like silk and he'll love touching you
- moisturize immediately after bathing—it seals in water that your skin has absorbed, taking years off aging skin
- light the candles around the tub while playing your favorite soft music

Lavish care on yourself. Enjoy yourself to the fullest. Forget all the negatives and lift up your spirits. Begin to think good thoughts about yourself, and enjoy, enjoy, enjoy. Remember that cold-water baths are refreshing; warm-water baths are soothing; hot-water baths are relaxing.

5. CHAMPAGNE BATH

This is more erotic when bathing with your lover. Bring a chilled bottle of champagne to your hot tub or bath. As you bathe, sip the champagne. Pour at least half into your tub, sip on some, and play with the rest. During that time dream up the most sensuous thing that you're going to do to your lover. Just talking and laughing adds to the pleasures of the champagne bath. Pouring small trickles down his back or on his chest while bathing is quite refreshing.

❧

Have a Sunday kind of love.

❧

19

Sexuality

Okay, let's dive right in. A woman spends a great deal of her days and nights being aware of her sexuality. She moistens and throbs on some occasions involuntarily. As a result of all she has learned from other women and friends her age, she is impressed that her sex is a bonafide point of leverage that can be used to get her way with men.

A woman uses her sexuality to entice men and will often present the intensity of her sexual desire to get his attention. A Real Woman lays sexual bait for her prey and will behave seductively when she is alone with a man she is trying to lure.

Women adore men, and getting them into bed is part of the fun. Once a woman sets out to get a man, she goes all out to bait him in. Of course, the spark of it all is to succeed in getting the prize (him). Some men feel that a woman will try to lure him into bed so that she will have certain rights in his life. This is not necessarily true. Women connect sex and love. When a woman gives the ultimate to her man—her body—she has given her heart as well. A measure of this sex and love or at least romance shows that love is thought of as a part of bonding.

Women are romantic creatures, and in the presence of men their confidence will be either sky high or very low. In this section, I will focus on the higher levels of sexual self-esteem and your sexual appetite.

A truly sensuous woman, with a healthy sexual appetite:

- allows an open line of communication because she is a romantic creature
- should always feel beautiful and desirable
- does not believe everything a man tells her
- should accept compliments honestly making direct eye contact with the giver of the compliment, smiling, and giving a cordial thank-you
- should be able to accept phone calls, compliments, and flowers without feeling an obligation to have sex
- enjoys the attention that a man gives her but doesn't take advantage of his kindness or generosities
- doesn't give too much or too little of herself
- gives body language signals that send messages of sex and romance only to someone she is honestly interested in
- will get to know her sexual partner
- will learn to trust her man
- will believe in him
- will be very selective about her sexual partner
- won't make it a habit of blaming or accusing
- won't sleep and tell
- won't be pretentious during sex
- will tell him what feels good
- will tell him what feels painful
- will be open, honest, and friendly
- won't expect him to figure out what she enjoys sexually—she'll let him know
- won't use sex as a weapon against him by denying it to him
- won't use sex as a manipulative measure to get things
- won't use her vagina and body as an aspect of being that gives existence and value
- will promote herself in a positive way without sex
- will be able to touch, caress, stroke, and give lots of hugging daily to her partner
- will respect her lover
- will respect herself

- will try her best not to settle for less in any form or fashion
- tries to pick times that will accommodate both her and her partner, such as when she knows he's feeling positive or after a success or good news
- will remain playful and cuddle often
- will show that she values him when she's not involved in genital sex
- will make frequent positive sexual overtures
- will be creative and won't get angry just because he lacks sexual desire

Remember: Love travels fast, "sensuality outlives love."

❖ *Sexual Self-esteem*

What really is sexual self-esteem? Experts and their thousands of studies can't seem to agree on what sexual self-esteem is or how to measure it precisely. The definition of self-esteem is being satisfied with one's self, having confidence and pride in one's self. The experiences of feeling that you're worthy of happiness and capable of managing life's challenges creates positive self-esteem.

Naturally, women who were brought up to be modest about their talents and strengths might be less egotistical. For years, self-esteem tests have rated men higher than women. Yet women are now increasing their levels of sexual self-esteem by reading books like *Will the Real Women . . . Please Stand Up!* and they are becoming increasingly satisfied with themselves. Therefore, creating a "go-for-it" attitude defines a healthy level of self-esteem.

Success doesn't ensure self-esteem. Most women don't have enough of it and they don't like to talk about it, but each of them wants some of it. Women are considering self-esteem the universal fix when they obsess over alcohol, food, or love.

Self-esteem is elusive, changeable, difficult to get, and even more difficult to hold on to. Self-esteem is a lot like love. Women often go looking for it in the wrong places. Women attempt to bolster their sense from within. Self-esteem is more a reflection of our relationship to others. Self-esteem is that personal meter that we have built into us to detect—and to prompt us to avert—the threat of rejection. Think of your self-esteem as a fuel gauge on your vehicle. Most of us are busy driving around trying to keep the indicator from registering "empty."

When our self-esteem is low, the appropriate response is not to fix our inner selves but repair our standing in the eyes of others.

Many women admit having a lifelong struggle with themselves when their self-esteem is low, insufficient, or lacking. They express feelings of self-hate and self-doubt when their self-esteem is low. Beauty, money, and strength don't matter when a woman's self-esteem is insufficient.

The truth about self-esteem is that no one has everything that they want or need all the time, and the shortage of it affects different women in different ways. For some women, low self-esteem is a problem in love, friendship, adventure, and work. For other women, self-esteem is the inner power that allows them to function but refuses them the joy of their achievements and deletes the pleasures they could take from their success.

Because women struggle to become perfect at everything they set out to do, they feel like failures when they come up short in any areas of their life. As life goes on, women, no matter how successful, feel less than average. The average man thinks he's better than good, but the average woman never thinks she's good enough. Self-esteem goes back to childhood. Most of us have a great supply of self-esteem in the beginning. Every little accomplishment we have builds our self-esteem and every little failure chops off a piece of it.

As we go through life, the need for approval and the struggle to maintain our self-esteem is a constant battle. Your idea of self and the self you see in the mirror creates a challenge. This challenge is to see both selves plainly and clearly. Taking personal inventory of yourself is sometimes very difficult, but the road to feeling better about yourself begins with not trying to define your whole self. Instead, define small parts of you, a little at a time, and soon your whole self will become a clearer and brighter picture to reckon with.

Using the standard method, your sexual self-esteem can be calculated. Answer the following questions to calculate your sexual self-esteem.

1. I take a positive attitude toward myself.
   a. always=5
   b. often=4
   c. sometimes=3
   d. rarely=2
   e. never=1

2. How often do you have sex?
   a. every day=5
   b. 2 –3 times a week=4
   c. about once a month=3
   d. 1–2 times a month=2
   e. about 6 times a year=1

3. At times I think I am no good at all.
   a. always=1
   b. often=2
   c. sometimes-3
   d. rarely=4
   e. never=5

4. Rate your sex life.
   a. excellent=5
   b. very good=4
   c. good=3
   d. satisfactory=2
   e. poor=1

5. On the whole, I am satisfied with myself.
   a. always=5
   b. often=4
   c. sometimes=3
   d. rarely=2
   e. never=1

6. How often do you masturbate?
   a. once a day=5
   b. 3 –5 times a week=3
   c. 2 –3 times a month=2
   d. 3 –5 times a year=1

7. I feel really disgusted with myself.
   a. always=1
   b. often=2
   c. sometimes=3
   d. rarely=4
   e. never=5

8. Has your partner performed oral sex on you?
   a. yes, often=5
   b. yes, seldom=3
   c. yes, rarely=2
   d. no, never=1

9. I first had sexual intercourse when I was
   10–15 years old=1
   b. 16–21 years old=2
   c. 21–26 years old=3
   d. not sexually active =5

10. How many orgasms do you have in one lovemaking session?
    a. none=1
    b. one=2
    c. 2 or more=3

11. How many sexual partners have you had since your first sexual encounter?
    a. 1–3=5
    b. 4–6=3
    c. 7–10=2
    d. 11–20=1

12. What is your marital status? (just curious)
    a. single, living alone=1
    b. single, living with parent=2
    c. married=3
    d. separated=4
    e. divorced=5
    f. widowed=6

Add up the numbers to your answers. If the total is less than 24, you have low self-esteem. If your number equals 25 or more, you have pretty good to high self-esteem. There really are no right or wrong answers to your self-esteem scores on this test. Good or bad self-esteem depends on how you feel at any given time.

The percentage of women who score high on self-esteem are presently 34 percent. Women who score medium are 21 percent and women who score low are 45 percent.

Women who experienced sexual intercourse with more than one sexual partner felt more confident and enjoyed their freedom to express themselves sexually. Women were asked their marital status simply to classify how many women within the survey were sexually active and were not married or had never been married.

If experts defined sexual self-esteem as how confident people feel about their relationships, women would outscore men:

- 56% of women compared to 41% of men feel they are a good friend
- 54% of women compared to 46% of men feel they are good workers
- 48% of women compared to 38% of men feel they are good parents
- 36% of women compared to 22% of men feel they are able to express emotions

In order of importance, there are the four keys to sexual self-esteem:

1. Satisfied with body and looks
2. Have paid work
3. See work as successful
4. Rate self as attractive

American women value independence, self-sufficiency, and uniqueness. In relationships, women have considerable strengths that often go unnoticed or unrewarded by the male-dominated society.

Being interdependent, seeing themselves in relation to other people, makes women feel good about themselves. If women had designed the presently used self-esteem test, men would be trying to explain their low opinion of themselves and how they should improve their self-image.

Even though 72 percent of women have a capacity to feel pity for others, it is difficult for them to feel sorry for themselves. As a group, women generally expect great things of themselves and are not tolerant of their own shortcomings. Feeling sorry for oneself is usually seen as negative, but it is in fact a key ingredient to a healthy self-esteem.

♦ *Lifters of Self-esteem*

1. Be real. Understand that you are good and your personal best is enough. Be able to feel good about your accomplishments—the large and the small.
2. Don't be controlled by material obsessions. Don't measure your self-worth by material obsessions or possessions. Be able to give to this world your love and help in ways other than material.
3. Create success in your life. Be able to put yourself in high gear when you are feeling low. There should be something good in your life to reflect on to raise your spirits in down times. Believe you are successful and you will become successful.
4. Review your personal successes. It might be a small or large success, but relish in the fact that there are things you can pull out in times of need. Bring personal happiness into your life.
5. Keep a positive outlook on life. Don't allow bad things to create a bad mood that you can't get over. This is the best time to remember all the things that make you happy. Think of things that will help you to feel worthwhile.
6. Take the proper action. By working to achieve the goal that you have set, you are taking the proper action. Your self-esteem can't help but to improve when you are taking action to improve your life.
7. Maintain good health habits. Don't let negative images of yourself cause you to neglect your health and well-being. Feeling good does not always mean that you are healthy, so get regular checkups, eat healthy, and exercise daily.
8. Meditate daily or as often as needed. Think peaceful thoughts.

Bring inner peace into your life by thinking positive and pleasant thoughts. Love yourself, respect yourself, and think of all the good you can do to make this world a better place.

✿ Two Kinds of Women

The differences between women with high self-esteem and those who scored low on the traditional scale of self-esteem are that women with high self-esteem are likely to:

- feel in control of life almost all the time
- have power at home
- have power at work
- use talents to fullest
- feel creative
- feel satisfied with: motherhood, friendships, marriage or love life, spiritual life
- be a college graduate
- earn $30,000 or more

Women with low self-esteem are likely to:

- be overweight
- call themselves names
- agree that "no one knows the real me"

Women liked themselves better if they:

- got more exercise
- lost ten pounds or more
- were smarter
- earned more money
- got more respect from children
- were appreciated more by spouse
- got listened to more

During my interviews the women told me what they considered important reasons for liking themselves. They are:

- a good parent
- a good friend
- understanding
- loving
- faithful
- dependable
- able to forgive someone
- spiritual and believe in God

Women agree that family relationships are most important, but their work and friends were a close second.

✾ *Sexual Appetite*

Of course you relish sex. Most people who are sexually active have a sexual appetite. Many conversations between women and men have sexual overtones. As difficult as it is to believe, having sex is fun and can be pleasurable all the time. Any woman can experience a full and rewarding sexual appetite, especially if she has discovered her sexuality in a positive way. Statistically speaking, most women are said to reach their sexual prime between twenty-eight and thirty-five years of age. They either love to have sex or the idea of having sex.

A woman who has learned to be in tune with her sexual appetite and has the ability to understand her sexual moods is a woman who appreciates her body and the pleasures that can be attained from it.

Before women can begin to understand the value of their sexual appetites, they must get in tune with their sexual moods. Women should chart their wants, needs, and desires on a monthly calendar. I charted mine and found that three to four days before my period, I was dormant sexually and had no desire to be kissed or touched by my lover. This usually lasted two days, but as soon as my period began I was as horny as a toad. When you have to have sex and you get it when you want it, do you also masturbate? Are you sexually high in the mornings, low in the evenings? Do you find yourself waking up in the morning yearning for his caress or his penis? Are you most erotic around the fifth of the month? Do you find that fatigue or worry make you want to cuddle with him? When alert and happy, do you want to make love all day long? When you drink alcohol, do you want romance more than sex? Do you prefer wild, passionate sex whether romance is present or not? Do you know which kisses turn you on and which ones turn you off? If you've never charted these things or haven't paid attention to your sexual senses, begin today by keeping personal records of your body's moods and sexsitivities. You'll be surprised at what you learn about yourself. Keep the chart for three to four months; the things that you've never paid attention to will begin to signal your sexual awareness.

After a few times with your lover, chart your sexual desires, your dislikes and likes. Record your ups and downs, your highs and lows. Rate your sexual partner from one to five. This is your own personal rating. He never has to know he's being rated. No one can tell you what is good and what is bad. It's all up to your own sexual appetite and what it takes to please you and *you only*. Everyone responds differently, so don't expect your sensitivity rate to be the same as your best friend, your sister, or anyone else. Jot down the times of day that your body is most responsive or most sexually excited. If you are dedicated to listening to your body's responses, you will awaken your body's sexual aptitude and you will learn how to read your body's sexual signals. This will enable you to appreciate yourself and to use your sexual appetite as long as you are sexually active. Besides, think of all the sexual pleasures that are awaiting you. Ummmmmm, just the thought of it all feels good.

❦ Sexual Myths

In a basically good relationship, having little or no sex may be an important factor or problem. Sometimes you'll have it all; most of the time you won't. Too bad, but it won't be the end of the world. Relationships come and go. Good ones as well as bad ones.

Sexual taboos, myths, and lies that may be getting in the way of stimulating a better relationship with your partner can be dispelled. Some sexual myths are:

Myth #1:   Automatic arousal is necessary before sex is enjoyed.

Fact: Sexual arousal is stimulated by fondling, touching, rubbing, kissing, and a possibly erotic mental image. Failure to focus on your sensory input can interfere with arousal due to negative thinking or distractions.

Myth #2:   Sex should not be scheduled.

Fact: If sex is spontaneous fine, but if, during the course of a busy day, it can't be spontaneous, scheduling is the next best thing. At least you can plan the romance and the atmosphere when it takes place. Anything you think is worth doing can be scheduled and preplanned.

Myth #3:   You can't get turned on by a best friend or a sibling.

Fact: Bull! If you lack imagination this might be true, but it's a natural part of evolution to be thrilled by someone you already know quite well. You can get turned on by thoughts of someone other than your lover as you make love to your lover. All that's needed is a little imagination and initiative.

Myth #4:   Intercourse is the ultimate to sexual satisfaction. Anything else does not count as good sex.

Fact: Sexual relations involve physical contact, whether it be touching fingers, toes, ears, eyes, or mouth. Erogenous zones are all over the body and to enjoy sex does not mean that you must be penetrated. You can experience physical connections and sensuality when you snuggle, hug, or hold hands. Erotic sex, intercourse, and orgasms are options that could create pleasurable consequences. Emphasis on these things will create sexual dysfunctions in a man who is trying desperately to slow his orgasm with a woman who is hurrying to get hers.

Myth #5:   If one person is turned on, lovemaking can be just as satisfying.

Fact: Pleasure is possible if only one person is turned on but only if the partner isn't resentful. It's acceptable for one person to be aroused by stimulation from the other without both partners being aroused. Even if both partners are sharing in the love, every lovemaking session can be successful. Not every session will be fulfilling for both partners every time no matter how many times you make love.

Myth #6:   It's unwise and artificial to try out new things.

Fact: Trying new and refreshing things is one of the best ways to keep love, romance, and sensuality alive and steamy in a relationship. Each partner should participate in the process of implementing new and wonderful things in their romance. If only a few of your sensuous physical experiments produce erotic sensations—*fantastic*! By increasing the ways you expand your sex life you can keep it exciting and refreshing.

Myth #7:   If a woman takes the lead in sex it can damage her partner's ego.

Fact: Men and women are more flexible and free in their lovemaking these days. If men tell themselves that a woman is too aggressive for taking the lead, then they might well believe that this is so. Anxiety might result, which, in turn, can cause decreased sexual enjoyment.

Myth #8:   Overweight partners are unattractive and you can't get turned on by them.

Fact: Making love to someone with a gorgeous body doesn't guarantee sexual satisfaction. An overweight person can be sensuous, romantic, and great in bed, whereas a person with a beautiful body can be lousy because he's stuck on himself. Some people with the most beautiful bodies are sexually gratifying. Many times, an overweight person will work extra hard to please his partner because of his lack of so-called body qualities.

Myth #9:   Having sexual fantasies about anyone other than your mate is abnormal and disgusting.

Fact: Sexual fantasies can be triggered by a variety of stimuli, including the way your partner touches, smells, thinks, or just about anything else. There isn't one particular thing or reason that brings sexual fantasies to the surface. The significance of it all can be quite rewarding. Women have sexual fantasies to increase or enhance their sexual experiences. Although some fantasies may be considered weird or bizarre, they should not be seen as abnormal or disgusting. Some people even see them as cheating, but who's to say what is really cheating!

Myth #10: Having to tell your partner what you want isn't necessary. You shouldn't have to touch yourself at all.

Fact: Many women feel that if they have to touch themselves or tell their partner what they want it means they are inadequate or not sensuous as a lover. This is not true, because each partner's brain is tied into his or her own physical sensations. The secret of good sex is to share specifics of likes and dislikes without judgment or criticisms during lovemaking. Keep experimenting to learn exactly what your lover wants most. Once you've learned the things that turn your partner on, it can be of tremendous value to enhancing your arousal and orgasmic threshold.

Myth #11: Sex should be man on the top, woman on the bottom to get full satisfaction.

Fact: Sex can be enjoyed in many different positions.

Myth #12: You have to be available to make love to him whenever he wants.

Fact: Forcing yourself to make love when you aren't in the mood is wrong. It only brings resentment into your lovemaking. Keeping him interested even when you don't feel like it is the best remedy. Don't neglect him or tell him that you don't feel like it; always make him feel desirable.

Myth #13: All men want sex.

Fact: Men want more than sex. They want physical, emotional, and mental stimulation from their lover. Kissing, hugging, and touching is quite sufficient for many men.

Myth #14: You can't teach an old lover new skills in the bed.

Fact: Most women confess that their lovers are willing to try new and exciting things in bed simply because they want to experience new things also.

Myth #15: Bad sex is better than none at all.
    Fact: Bad sex is *not* better than no sex, because bad sex can compound negative feelings.

Myth #16: Men like sexually aggressive women.
    Fact: Men like sensuous women who flirt, tantalize, and tease. But once initial contact is made, they prefer women to step back and let them take over. They don't want women who take over the relationship.

Myth #17: Older couples have the best sex.
    Fact: Older women do have an advantage because they are often in tune with their sexuality. This does not necessarily mean that they have the best sex; they do, however, have sexual wisdom in many cases. Getting in tune takes a little longer for some women.

There are many, many more myths circulating in the sexual arena, maybe you've even heard a few that caught your attention. The most important thing to remember about myths: acknowledge them and communicate with your lover as you experiment. Revitalize your lovemaking as you revitalize your life and have fun in love as well as in lovemaking.

❀ Sexual Ethics

Every sexually active woman must take responsibility for her sexual actions. There will be many times that she will want to spread her legs and get involved with a man who's not right for her.

Good judgment is necessary to keep dignity as well as integrity intact. Since ethics are a very personal thing, a woman should consider them one of her most important personal assets. The code of sexual ethics relates to your entire approach to sexual encounters. Every woman has secret codes that she caters to as she sets her standards. Having a conscience should also serve as a part of your code of sexual ethics. Here are a few to get you started in the right direction. Add to this list as you develop your own code of ethics.

1. DON'T BE A GOSSIP

Sexual gossip can hurt the woman more. Sex should be beautiful, therefore your sexual habits are to be cherished and remembered as such. Don't allow your ego to spoil your pleasures by gossiping.

2. KEEP YOUR HANDS OFF YOUR BEST FRIEND'S MAN

Don't flirt or send out sexual signals to a man you know belongs to one of your friends. If, on the other hand, you want to end the friendship, go for it. However, this is not something Real Women do. People have feelings.

3. DON'T GIVE IN SENSUOUSLY TO MEN YOU DON'T WANT

Don't get in the habit of letting men touch you who have no feelings for you, even if he's your husband.

4. GIVE TO HIM COMPLETELY IF YOU LOVE HIM

If you honestly love him, give yourself to him, completely. If he's the type who disrespects you or belittles you and is bad for you, dump him.

5. DON'T FALL IN LOVE WITH MARRIED MEN

This one is easier said than done. He's probably the dreamboat you've been looking for all your life, but he's married and you can't have him—or can you? There are plenty of fine, single men who want loving and are willing to give good loving in return. Married men can't sleep over, it's difficult for them to go away weekends, and they have limited activities to share with you. Even married women can't completely enjoy an affair with a married man, but it does have its benefits. The expectations are equal and not as one-sided as in an affair where one partner is married and the other isn't.

6. DON'T TEASE OR LEAD A MAN ON IF YOU DON'T WANT HIM

If there is no physical or emotional attraction to him, don't play games with his emotions. Why mistreat, torture, or tease a man that you don't want or have no intentions of loving.

7. DON'T TELL A MAN YOU LOVE HIM IF YOU DON'T

Don't lie to him in order to get screwed, to test his masculinity, or to get his money. I know that when a woman sets out to get a man, she will do whatever she can to get him, but don't tell him you love him, especially if he's emotionally too weak for you. And if you can't have your way with him, don't sink so low that you say "I love you" just to get your way. Being a Real Woman does not give you the right or privilege to hurt other people's feelings. You don't get a permit to do as you please. You *must* develop a logical set of ethics that are personal, positive, and practical enough to follow. Keep them clear in your mind; whatever you decide is right or wrong will help to guide you in the right direction. You'll be better off in your sexual relationships. You'll save yourself grief and guilt trips down the road.

8. DON'T EXPECT HIM TO PROVIDE THE ONLY MEANS OF BIRTH CONTROL

A smart woman will also provide the necessary protection to avoid an unwanted pregnancy as well as sexually transmitted diseases.

9. TAKE RESPONSIBILITY FOR WHAT YOU WANT

Society's idea about what's nice and what isn't nice has caused many women to miss out on what they really desire. The only way some women can escape this trap is when things develop in a way that just happens. Unfortunately, reasons to accept compromised feelings without looking anxious and without taking responsibility for what might happen occur more often in the world of fiction than in real life. We have to face the fact that sometimes we want to do things that are inappropriate to our own and society's standards. When we try to figure out who actually benefits from our conventional behaviors, most of the time no one does. Don't allow a lack of courage to keep you from doing what you really want to do.

10. Don't Project Negative Signals

A realistic woman knows that meeting the man she wants cannot be left to chance. She has to do her part in communicating that she is available. She should not be so distant that a man chooses to bypass her because of her negative persona. If a woman gives off the right signals and keeps an open mind toward men, she can project the right signals to land the man of her choice.

11. Don't Discourage Men from Approaching You

When you see a man you like, and he really turns you on, it's up to you as a woman to go a step further and encourage him in a positive way to come closer. A man still chases a woman until she catches him, but if she doesn't encourage him along the way he'll feel rejected and give up on the chase. Showing him that you are ready and willing is where a relationship often starts. A willing woman is difficult for a man to resist.

12. Don't Deprive Him of the Chance to Spoil and Want You

Once you know that he wants you, relax and enjoy the results of your work and the continued efforts of his work. Give him the opportunity to spoil you. Most men enjoy the idea and the efforts involved in pampering a woman. For a man, it's important to impress a woman, anytime and anywhere. A woman should never offer to pay for half of the meal she just enjoyed. Even if you earn just as much or more, there is no reason you can't adore his generosity. Enjoy all of his admiration and give him the proper time to desire you by giving him the proper attention. Let him be uncertain whether you will make love to him when you two finally get together.

13. BE SURE THAT WHAT YOU GET IS WHAT YOU WANT

Insecurities, disappointments, and doubts often make women settle for less than they deserve. When you find a man you are attracted to, don't let your feelings run away with you. Try to be cool; and don't get overanxious about him. Don't ever feel that you are lucky to have him. Remember that he should feel lucky to have you. Look at where you are, and why you are there, and then be grateful that you have a right to make your own decisions and choices in a relationship. Pay attention to the initial stages of the relationship so that failure can be avoided. Let your mind speak as clearly as your feelings. This will assist in preventing future pain and suffering down the road.

❦

Be honest with yourself.

❦

20

Vagina

❧ Your Sexiest Asset ❧

One of the most popular words in the world is "vagina." This tiny yet powerful lovemaker has a scent that can weaken the strongest men. Just the thought of it can stiffen men to long, hot grunts. The pride of most men is this wonderful and fantastic orifice.

Between a woman's legs is the most fascinating of all human organs. The vagina is the true tunnel of love. Many girls don't appreciate its size, but a woman will treasure its mere presence. This tiny hole, which enlarges as a man's erect penis enters it, is a pleasure center to be adored by all who possess one. The muscles that make up the vaginal walls have the capacity to hold onto your lover's penis as it enters you. It is called the barrel of the vagina and it is heaped with muscles that are crucial to pleasing a man.

Youth brings tight, taut, and gripping resistance. Growing older and bearing children causes these muscles to become loose and slack. Men prefer tighter vaginas. Rest assured there are ways to keep it tight and trim to please the both of you.

❧ Exercising the Vagina

One of the best ways to keep the vagina tight and trim is to exercise it. No matter what you're doing or where you are, you can contract the vaginal muscles for at least an hour or so each day. Controlling vaginal muscles will become easier if you exercise them regularly. Developing the snatching motion with these muscles will increase your lover's appreciation and excitement. But keeping the muscles in shape takes time, practice, and consistency.

Practice can be great if you can find a plastic, penis-shaped vibrator or another hard object that is approximately the same size as a man's penis. Insert the newfound object into your vagina and, using only your muscles, begin to squeeze inward. Be sure to clean the object thoroughly before using. Continue to do this exercise daily until you can shoot the object out of you like a fired bullet. Set a goal of shooting it ten feet. Once your vaginal muscles have been trained, they are very powerful.

Some women have trained their muscles to the firmness of echoing musical tunes. Some have even toned their vaginal muscles to the tightness of squirting fluids up to thirty feet, or picking up coins from the floor. You may not want to develop your vaginal muscles to this point, but it sure can work wonders in bed. Having a tight and trim vagina to accompany your lovemaking is great for your lover also.

When a man's penis comes in contact with your vagina, you can use your vagina to caress him, stimulate him, excite him, control him, and eventually bring him to a climax. Getting your vaginal muscles into shape should be one of your most important missions as a sensuously attractive woman. The next thing to do is operate them as sensuously as you possibly can.

A man will feel many sensations in his penis as he enters your vagina. When the head of his penis (the glans) bumps its way past your inner lips, or your labia minora, it becomes easily swollen with blood, causing sexual excitement. As the male plunges his penis into your vagina, he feels a soft, wet, warm, and clinging sensation on the entire length of his penis. Practicing your vaginal exercises on his penis will bring him wonderful sensations.

❧ *Vaginal Muscles*

When your vaginal muscles are flexed, he will feel a sensation on his penis somewhat like a small hill with a speed bump. As he receives full stimulation from making love, a combination of sensations are felt by you: swollen labia minora, moist vaginal interior, extra tantalization from your taut vaginal muscles, and suction from your hungry vaginal muscles.

Your muscles will contract when you reach a climax. The contractions that you feel he also feels, which should be pleasurable for both of you. When a woman climaxes, she doesn't squirt her fluids as a man does, she secretes liquid from her vaginal walls.

The vagina has a distinct smell to it that is perfectly normal. A woman should worry if she doesn't have a smell, because the purpose of fresh vaginal odor is to arouse a man. Many women find it hard to believe, but what really turns a man on is the smell of a well-lubricated vagina. Women who use deodorants would be doing themselves a sexual disfavor as well as possible harm to the sensitivity of the vaginal tissues. Your freshness should be attractive, not offensive or old. The myth that vaginas smell like fish started because of an unclean vagina.

Secretions from the vagina are clear or slightly milky. Anything else deserves a check from your doctor. Lubrication for comfortable lovemaking can be used to stimulate the flow of vaginal secretions.

❧ *Vaginal Sensations*

Sometimes words are not enough when discussing sexual organs. All women should have enough nerve to pose naked in front of their mirrors. They should examine themselves in great detail. Many women give men that privilege before they've taken it themselves.

Sit or lie down with your legs spread apart. The part of the vagina that is first visible is the vulva. Separate your vulva (outer lips) as far as you possibly can. At the lower section of your vaginal lips is the entrance to the vagina, which is where the penis penetrates during intercourse. The internal lips are called the labia minora; these become engorged with blood and swell to a beautiful puffy fullness when sexually aroused. Above the vagina is the urethra, which is a very tiny opening. Above the urethral opening is a pyramid-shaped hood formed by the meeting of the lips. Within these lips is a pea-shaped bump called the clitoris. Whether your clitoris is large or small you do have one. Many people have difficulty finding it because of its hidden quality, especially men.

Just as a man has a penis, a woman has a clitoris. When a woman is aroused, it gets swollen, just as a man's penis does. It gets swollen stiff and very sensitive. The clitoris is a small part of a large organ, which is hidden inside the female. Stimulating the clitoris physically turns women on and, whether direct or indirect, stimulation causes excitement in this tiny sex organ. The excitement comes with penile penetration as your lover slides in and out of your vagina, rubbing up against your clitoris or brushing his pubic hairs against it. This leads to pleasant sensations as it pulls on the labia minora and against the clitoris.

The simple pressure of a man's pubic bone is enough stimulation to excite a woman to a climax. Most women can use direct stimulation to bring themselves to an orgasm. This is called masturbation. The problem is not with women bringing orgasms to themselves, it is with whether or not men can stimulate the clitoris properly enough to bring a woman to orgasm.

Before any woman can expect a man to bring her to those fantastic and glorious sensations she must be able to bring herself to orgasmic heights. Besides, how can a woman tell a man where to touch her if she doesn't know.

You can help your partner by guiding him through the art of satisfying you by using masturbation techniques. It takes years for some women to find their clitoris. When they finally discover this pleasure button, they are ecstatic. Some useful ways for lovers to share in stimulation are:

1. sexual devices called clitoral simulators that help arouse
2. tongue kissing the clitoris
3. vibrators
4. massagers
5. rubbing or self-stimulation
6. having your mate rub your clitoris
7. water from a faucet running onto your clitoris

Don't stimulate your clitoris every day manually or during love-making or it will become difficult to climax with direct stimulation. Getting this extra boost is nice, but don't allow clitoral stimulation to be your only way of achieving essential satisfaction in sex. It will eventually become a nuisance. Whether your clitoris is large or small has no bearing on your erotic stimulation.

❧ Vaginal Tricks and Palpitations

Oh . . . the things you can do with those vaginal muscles. Some women think that in order to climax you have to be manually stimulated by your lover. This is far from the truth. If you are having sexual intercourse and all you're receiving is a sore vagina, I don't need to tell you something's wrong. Things don't have to be this way.

Every woman has a sex sense, but it must be trained, just like your other senses, through exercise. With practice, you learned to dance on beat. With practice, you will also learn to control the rhythm of your vaginal muscles. Using the proper vaginal palpitations will add tantalizing sensations to your lover's penis. To help you build up your confidence in your sexual ability, your sexual senses must be greatly enhanced.

The vaginal tricks used to practice your palpitations were all designed by women who have tried and tested their methods. These palpitations will help to bring additional pleasures while making love.

Number one: When douching, place the vaginal syringe at the tip of your vagina and with the suction of your vagina squeeze and pull the syringe in using only your muscles. If you are doing this properly, your vagina will act as a vice and grip the syringe as it cleanses your vagina. It will simultaneously suction water from the syringe and cleanse you. You can practice this method each time you douche, so you'll get vagina exercises to improve palpitations even while cleansing.

Number two: While masturbating, suction your vaginal muscles in and out as tightly as you can. This method adds sensitivity and stimulation to your clitoris as you masturbate. The suctions and palpitations strengthen your vaginal walls, thereby increasing the gripping tendencies of all your vaginal muscles.

❧

Think of silk when you touch your mate.

❧

21

Discovering Your Clitoris

❦ Pleasures ❦

*I*f you really enjoy having your clitoris stimulated, then this chapter is for you. Even though many women enjoy clitoral stimulation, most prefer indirect stimulation by gentle, circular motions from the hand or tongue. Imagine these movements surrounding the clitoris as he rhythmically plays with it. Stimulating the clitoris helps women to achieve orgasms. Even though men are still confused about the actual location of the clitoris and how it should be touched, they manage to find its vicinity. With all the publicity surrounding the clitoris, it's no wonder men as well as women worship it. Even the unsureness of its complete function brings excitement. Stimulation to the clitoris directly or indirectly has helped many women achieve orgasms during sexual intercourse. Men feel that they can make a woman come without direct clitoris stimulation, whereas most women surveyed felt that the stimulation was needed to achieve an orgasm.

Indications are that the clitoris is still a mystery in spite of all the articles and research done to explain its significance, location, and stimulant requirements. Men don't seem to understand how to proceed since women fake orgasms. Men are mystified by the clitoris and fear that they are too rough or not rough enough, and they sometimes feel that they are not manly enough to bring their women to orgasms with their penis.

Don't continue to deny your needs to yourself or your lover. If you want your clitoris stimulated you must let your lover know. If you are close enough to be having sex, then you're close enough to ask for what you want from your lover.

Few men will admit that they experience difficulty finding a woman's love button. To find the clitoris, use this simple method: *show him.* Since many men feel uncomfortable asking for directions to the clitoris, the woman should show him as a natural part of lovemaking. A woman has a personal right to show her lover what she wants. Have the man pull away the fleshy part of the labia with one hand and as he wets his finger he should begin circular motions alternating with a back and forth motion. If he uses this motion he won't miss any part of your clitoris. You may be a little shy at first, but after the initial showing and guiding of his hand, you'll feel more comfortable. Even though everyone is different, men naturally seek out the easiest approach. This approach usually works on most women.

Once a woman has become acquainted with clitoral stimulation she craves it. One of the most popular clitoral stimulations is the use of your lover's tongue in long, slow horizontal strokes along the sides of the clitoris. The hand is usually the least popular stimulant because the hand tends to be rough and without constant lubrication; it can scratch or scuff the clitoris. The tongue is nicer because it is naturally lubricated and it's also softer. The tongue can get into tiny crevices of the clitoral area that are difficult for the finger to manipulate. Lubrication is very important to the clitoris. Even if the hand is lubricated, it doesn't seem to manipulate or stimulate the clitoris as well as the mouth or tongue.

The use of the tongue is almost always sure to turn you on. The hand and finger pressure is often a negative factor with the main complaint being they are either too rough or not hard enough. Some men have learned to combine their hand, finger, and mouth stimulations. This method is one of the most effective ways of stimulating the clitoris. By using the middle finger to make soft figure-eight motions, a man can drive a woman to ecstasy. He can kiss her back while stimulating her clitoris. He can kiss her stomach, navel, and breast as he stimulates her clitoris.

Other methods can also be tried. He can nibble, lick, or bite her buttocks while stimulating her clitoris.

The best methods of all are those that you and your lover invent. Don't allow him to cause you pain or discomfort while trying to please you. The clitoris is very sensitive and some women do not like or need direct stimulation.

Most women I interviewed liked direct clitoral stimulation. Women who enjoy clitoral stimulation can enjoy it even more if they guided their lovers in the right direction. Now that you know the penis is not the ultimate satisfier and the clitoris is the key to a woman's orgasm, we can give the clitoris its fully deserved credit. Don't become a my-time-your-time lovemaker. Become a total part of your sexual delight, whether through manual or oral stimulation. Help your lover bring you to the edge of climax, then stop and allow him to use his hand, finger, or mouth before he makes love to you. You'll be so hot that the grinding and rubbing will bring each of you off. The main thing is to get yours first and then to help him to get his as you get yours again. Believe in yourself, believe in your orgasms, and believe that your pleasures are natural, needed, and beneficial.

Good performance is lasting.

22

Penis

*T*he penis is the basic area on a man that can be counted on to bring fantastic sensations. Most women know that this area is full of sensitive nerve endings.

Between your man's masculine legs is this fabulous, extraordinary, and powerful piece of 100 percent beef. Many myths surround this infamous piece of meat. The mere presence of a man will cause some women to discreetly eye the bulge in his pants. Though it has many names (penis, dick, cock, dingus, wang, pecker, toolie, john, willie, and thing), they all stand for the same erotic object of a woman's desire.

Actually, to a Real Woman, the actions and proportions of the penis are not difficult to understand, nor is the penis difficult to interpret. The penis is simply nothing more than a rounded, lengthy sponge that fills when sexually aroused. Inside the shaft of the penis is a network of spongy tissues that fill up with blood. There is a valve that restricts the blood from leaving the penis too soon. This causes the shaft to become hard and swollen, which, in turn, creates an erection. The rounded head of the penis, also known as the fireman's helmet because of its shape, is full of sensitive nerve endings that respond to rubbing. The most sensitive part of this organ is the frenum, a thin piece of skin located behind the opening at the tip of the penis.

Male sperm is produced in the testicles, which some people know as the nuts or balls, located in the pouch that hangs beneath the penis. The purpose of them dangling freely in the breeze is because the production of sperm requires temperatures lower than normal body temperature. The balls are wrinkled because that helps to radiate heat away from the balls, helping to keep them cool. When cooled, your man's balls may tighten and shrink. This is because heat is retained by the scrotum.

Sperm made by the testicles later proceed up a tube where the seminal fluid is produced. The sperm is protected and nourished here. When your lover is stimulated, this fluid goes into the tube that runs up the middle of the penis. The sensations trigger a muscular reaction of spasms. The semen then comes out in about four squirts that can sometimes travel as far as ten feet or more.

The bladder is closed off during erection of the penis, so simultaneous ejaculation and urination is impossible. Erections don't actually hurt, but they do feel tingly and swollen to men. Some men have morning erections known as morning glory. This erection is caused by a full bladder and should not be considered an erotic interlude.

As many things that can cause an erection can cause a loss of one. Alcohol can make a man feel enlarged but can cause "brewers droop." Narcotics and tranquilizers do the same. Anxiety and tension can also cause a limp penis, so to speak.

If your man experiences penis downfall, reassure him that all is okay by continuing to give love and affection. Don't complain or criticize him about his inability to get an erection. Joking isn't nice nor is it appropriate. Be tolerant of him and soon his penis will once again be erect.

If his penis still doesn't grow, encourage him in a positive and hopeful way to see a doctor. Trying to increase his penile erection with gadgets may cause him to grow dependent on them without resolving his problem.

❦ Penis Size

The average length of the penis is about six inches when erect. The longest penis in the world is recorded as fourteen inches. It was last seen in the East African bush. Penises vary greatly in length, width, and shape; plus, some are straight when erect, and others curve back or sideways. Your vagina will be able to accommodate an average penis plus a few inches more. After all, babies come from this opening. You'll have no trouble fitting your lover even if he looks larger with a hard on.

Some men have anxiety problems because they feel that their penises are too small. Both women and men take the value and size of penises very seriously. What they fail to realize, however, is no matter how small, large, or well hung a man's penis, the size is not really a factor in sexual intercourse. The size of a man's penis is not a problem for the woman who knows that she can be equally satisfied by any penis as long as the man who owns it knows how to use it. Since so many women tend to worry about the tightness of their vagina or the size of their breasts, the least of their worries is the size of their man's penis.

Penis size has become a tiresome obsession. The man who carries the lightest load between his legs is usually embarrassed by it and feels insecure on most occasions. If your man thinks his penis is too small, don't allow him to hassle with hormones, vacuum pumps, or other contraptions, because they have been proven not to work for enlargement, although they have been known to build a man's ego.

Don't let your man pad his crotch; false advertising will hardly relieve his insecurities. It will only cause disappointment later. The woman can play an important role in helping her lover to recognize the other good aspects of his penis size. Obsession with size only serves to reduce a man to a statistic, and society is already too preoccupied with the quantity of human beings. Whatever the size of the penis, it is worthy of its limited functions, and it is fully capable of giving you pleasure if your vagina is not too big.

A French army surgeon named Dr. Jacobus Sutor made a survey of penis size in Africa at the end of the nineteenth century. He went from village to village measuring the penis of any man who gave him consent. My question is how did this doctor feel measuring all those dicks?

Facts About Penis Size:

Some important facts for women to remember when they get too preoccupied with penis size are:

1. A man's penis size in its dormant state is not much smaller than in its erect state, and a small penis in its dormant state is usually bigger in its erect state.
2. No matter what the size of his penis, that is not the only tool used to arouse a woman. To be honest, penises aren't really good for anything but poking sensuously in and out of you. They are inflexible when hard, and they have no protruding surfaces.
3. When making love to a woman, a man's most effective sexual organs are his hands and tongue. Whatever the size of your man's penis, it's deserving of its limited functions and it's fully capable of giving a woman the pleasures it was meant to give.

Once a woman realizes that her man is not sexually limited physically, he'll have to stop giving her lame excuses for not being able to be a complete sexual partner. He'll have to also rid himself of those self-defeating feelings of inadequacy that have deprived her of sexual fulfillment.

Practice will help you to find out how firmly he wants to be caressed or touched. You should also keep in mind that the head of his penis is the most sensitive area and it will respond to various degrees of pressure. The penis shaft has less sensitivity to it, so you can grip it, clasp it, or caress it with more strength. Men feel that women don't hold their penises with enough firmness when fondling or masturbating them. The tennis racket hold is said to be a good feeling. If you want your partner to really respond to your touching of his penis you should grasp with a tightening grip as you descend toward the base of his penis (see Penis Exercises, page 131).

❦ *Circumcised vs. Uncircumcised*

Circumcision, an operation meaning "to cut around," has been performed for ritualistic rather than for medical reasons. The Old Testament interprets circumcision as the "blood of life sacrifice," and many traditions of circumcision derive from religious beliefs rather than hygienic concerns.

During the Roman Empire, a foreskinned, uncircumcised, or draped penis, although important cosmetically, was the subject of great controversy. Men who participated in athletic games were required to have foreskin covering the glans, or head of the penis, to reduce the penis's sensitivity. Contrary to this practice, many athletes who came from North Africa and the eastern Mediterranean, where circumcision was common, were required to have the foreskin replaced before they could participate in athletic activities, the logic being that Real Men participated in athletic games. In these areas of the world, circumcision was considered a symbol of power in the male hierarchy. Within the family structure, the father was the most powerful and, therefore, dominant member of the household, and many boys were not circumcised until they reached maturity.

Circumcision was practiced from the time of the Roman Empire because many physicians believed that it prohibited masturbation. In fact, circumcision increases the penis's sensitivity because the nerve endings are not killed, as was the intention, but more exposed and vulnerable to the touch. In the nineteenth century, circumcision became popular in the United States for similar reasons. Today, circumcision serves no medical purpose, although it has been suggested as useful as a hygienic measure. A circumcised penis is thought to be easier to keep clean, but to clean an uncircumcised penis you would need to spend only a few seconds to get it tidy. When erect, circumcised and uncircumcised penises look and feel practically the same.

Sixty-two percent of the women I interviewed said they wouldn't dare perform oral sex on an uncircumcised penis. This same group of women felt that an uncircumcised penis was unattractive and unsexy. This group also felt that it carried an odor that was not very enticing when making love.

Some men will experience the lack of a full erection due to the foreskin being too tight. This condition is called phimosis. Medical circumcision is required when the foreskin is too tight, which is sometimes caused by recurring infections.

Circumcision of an adult male can be very painful and serious and should not be undertaken purely for cosmetic reasons. Trying to circumcise oneself can result in mutilation and very serious infections.

If you happen to fall in love or even decide to make love to an uncircumcised penis, here are a few things you should remember:

1. Keep condoms available at all times and use them, whether he is circumcised or uncircumcised. It's for the health of it.
2. Make sure your lover pulls the foreskin back and cleans himself thoroughly with soap and water. You may choose to assist him in this effort on occasions so that he will be assured of your support.
3. If his penis possesses odors that are unfamiliar, refuse to have sex until he investigates why.
4. Remember rules number one through three.

❀ *Female Circumcision*

Women can also be circumcised, although many people are unaware of it. There are several reasons for a woman to be circumcised:

1. She's unable to achieve an orgasm during intercourse because the hood or foreskin that covers the clitoris is too large. The foreskin or hood usually covers the clitoris in the same way that the penis is covered when it is uncircumcised. Having this hood removed does not guarantee an orgasm.
2. Western cultures perform female circumcisions for sexual reasons, but in parts of Africa and Egypt female circumcision is a religious custom. Circumcision qualifies a woman of these cultures to act as a man temporarily when the man is away from the family. It is based on practicality, not sexual consideration.

❀ *Penis Exercises*

Here are some penile exercises that are sure to bring more control and stamina to your man's penis.

1. Take a wet towel and wrap it around your man's penis. Have him practice lifting the wet towel with his penis. *No hands allowed.* You can count as he lifts or he can lift in private. The object is to

have him lift to a set number daily; after about a week or so, you should begin to notice his penile thrusts being more controlled and rhythmic as you make love. This control will heighten his pleasures. Have him practice lifting other objects with his penis. After all, it can only help.

2. Tell him that you have a special exercise just for him. Have him stand naked the length of his penis away from you. If his penis is four inches while soft, have him stand only four inches away. His objective is to try to touch you with his penis as he lifts it. He can't touch it with his hands, nor can you. He must lift to touch you twenty times in the beginning, and increase the lifts as often as needed. You may not make it to twenty before you want to have him make love to you, but try anyway.

A variation of this is to have him try to lift his penis to your mouth at least twenty times before you have sex. Kneel on your knees as he stands in front of you to play the game.

3. Spell your name on his penis as you administer oral sex. Here's how: Suppose his name is Joe Bob Baker, take your tongue, and as you suck, lick, or fondle him with your mouth, draw each letter on his penis with your tongue. Make each letter three or four times by drawing it different ways. First spell it in cursive writing, then block style, then print it. You can stay on each letter for as long as you like. Naturally, there will be some letters that you are writing out that will feel better than others to you and him.

A variation of this spelling game is to have him draw his name on your clitoris with the head of his penis or his tongue. Make it more interesting by writing the entire alphabet in cursive, block, or print style. If you know how to write in calligraphy, try it on his penis, and then let him return the favor on your clitoris. Incorporate your favorite writing skills to this game and the fun will be endless.

You can spell, draw, or even sculpt on his head with your tongue; think of all the good practice you'll be getting.

❦ *Floppy Dicks—Not Floppy Disks*

While women are concerned with their desirability as lovers, a man is asking himself several questions:

Will I be able to get an erection?
Will I be able to keep an erection?

Am I turning her on?
Did the last man she was with do it better?

In the past, women have passively opened their legs to subject themselves to their partners sexual affections only to be disappointed—to tears sometimes. Women are no longer willing to settle for *just sex*. Women want sensuality, emotion, and excitement from their partners. Women's capacity to have orgasm has caused an inferiority complex for men during sexual intercourse. Men fear the fact that women can have multiple orgasms compared to their one. The importance for men to be considered good lovers is obvious. A man's sexual self-esteem is related to orgasms and potency. Orgasm popularity has become somewhat of a burden to men, and to find out that most of what he's been doing to please a woman sexually was wrong makes him a little insecure.

With all the hang-ups men have about sex, it's a wonder they can get it up. By the time men get past their seductive stage and lure women to the bedroom, their devastation causes floppy dicks. Rather than express what's bothering them they'll say "This has never happened to me before." Some women feel that men avoided them after sexual problems occurred, and some women avoided men who didn't satisfy them on the first try.

If a man's penis says no, sexual intercourse is practically out of the question, so women should learn to give other forms of physical attention in times like these.

❖ *What to Do with His Penis (Skills)*

1. Roll his penis between the palms of your hands and knead it as if it were a piece of bread dough.
2. Press his penis against your pelvis.
3. Thump his penis against your belly, face, or thighs.
4. Allow him to rub his penis between the cheeks of your buttocks.
5. Fondle his testicles as you rub his penis.
6. Press your finger or your tongue on the area between his anus and his scrotum. This spot is called the perineum, and it stimulates his prostate.
7. Fondle him just because he's your man. While he's read-

ing, talking on the phone, cooking, or doing handy work around the house is a good time to reach into his pants and fondle him.

8. Make two rings with the thumb and index finger of each hand. Place them next to each other on the middle of his penis. Gently pull in opposite directions at once.

9. Without penetration, have him rub his penis over the entire surface of your vagina very slowly.

10. Press your breasts together and let him slide his penis between them. Rub your breasts across his body, stroking your nipples ever so lightly against his penis. He'll enjoy watching you manipulate his penis. A sensuous pleasure to top this would be to allow his penis to emerge from between your breasts to your mouth.

※

Make positive effort, even if you're not
sure of the outcome.

※

23

Great Balls of Fire

What to do with those balls. In all cases, where your lover's balls are concerned, the tongue provides one of the most important pleasures of all. Even though men like to have their balls gently stroked and caressed, they really like having them licked. There are various ways that you can do this without causing pain to this sensitive area.

❀ *Stimulation Techniques*

Some popular stimulation techniques applied to the balls are:

1. Stroking with the tongue from the underside to the topside.
2. Long to short licks and then long again.
3. Just barely place your massager or vibrator on the underside of his balls, making sure you gently pass his anus as you begin.

4. Gently cup his balls in the palms of your hands as you caress and lick, lick and caress.
5. Rub or lick from his anus to his balls over and over again throughout foreplay and then again right before sexual intercourse.
6. Gently blow on his balls as you lick them. The chill going onto his balls will send pleasurable chills up and down his spine.
7. Humming his favorite tune on his balls will give him erotic shivers. He won't be able to think of anything or anyone but you.

*Know that you are much more
than just your looks.*

24

Sex: What's Normal

The question that tends to come up the most about sex is "Am I normal?" Most women are concerned with the normality of their sexual fantasies, responses, preferences, turnoffs, secrets, and problems. Other concerns are the normality of their body features, and the frequency in which they want to have sex. The fear of being sexually abnormal can prevent pleasure and intimacy. Fear has consequences and is the basis for many versions of "Am I normal?" Women said things like:

My climax takes too long and that frightens me.
Should a man be able to keep an erection for a long time?
Do other people make love as often as I do?
Does the enjoyment of oral sex make me weird?

"Normal" means different things to different people. People worry about what is statistically common, what our culture says is the right or wrong way in sexual behaviors. Sexual norms have altered and changed within our lifetime. The acceptance of homosexuality, the clitoris, and even what is considered a wife's duties have all changed. Socially speaking, normal is what is socially accepted as normal by responsible consenting adults. What is not consensual is wrong, just as tricking someone into making love to you. Being irresponsible is also wrong. To expose a partner to a sexually transmitted disease is irresponsible, therefore it's wrong.

Society teaches children that sex is bad. Learning that sex is bad means that, as sexual beings, we are bad. These messages are derived from families, churches, synagogues, and schools. Our environment teaches a child that sensitivity is somewhat abnormal also. Withholding sexual information from our children until they are grown handicaps them. We want them to be intelligent, normal people, but when they are sexually confused about their erotic feelings, we blame the entertainment industry.

✸ Sexual Customs

The United States has many laws governing sexual behavior— more than all the European nations combined. The only legally sanctioned sexual act in the United States is private heterosexual intercourse between married adults.

Some societies have no words for indecent, obscene, or impure in their vocabularies. The topic of sex is not considered shameful or embarrassing.

Boys in Mangaia (one of the Cook Islands) are given sexual instructions and taught sexual techniques and various coital positions, breast stimulations, cunnilingus, and methods of delaying ejaculation so that their female partners may experience orgasms.

The inhabitants of Bali and India have no elaborate practices of seduction. If sex is desired, one needs simply to ask. The Aweikoma of Brazil feel that since eating and intercourse involve body orifices, the same term is used for both activities. Tinquian people of the Pacific Islands do not kiss, instead, they place their lips close to their partners' lips and rapidly inhale.

The National Center of Health reports that 70 percent of married women have had premarital sex and that 95 percent of American women have had sex by the age of twenty-five. Americans are exposed to some form of sexual innuendo about twelve times an hour or every five minutes.

This information was obtained from *The Complete Book of Sexual Trivia* by Leslie Welch.

❦ *What Is Too Much Sex*

You think about sex often. You've just got to have it every day. Could you be addicted to sex? Wanting to sleep with an attractive stranger or even doing so does not make you a nymphomaniac, nor does the fact that you slept with an old boyfriend. In some of the worst relationships sex is sometimes the last thing to go sour. Don't blame yourself for enjoying sex. Blame your sexual addiction on the new concept and overpublicized trend of sexual dysfunctions. Nationwide treatment for sex addicts is not unusual. Many self-help groups that operate using the twelve-step program are now forming. Sex addiction is considered a new disease and its treatments tend to make perfectly healthy women feel guilty just for having normal sexual desires. *Don't!*

❦ *Sexual Confessions*

Addicts are usually very easy to get into bed. Some of the things that tend to turn a sexual addict on are:

- Tying wrists and ankles together or to the bedposts. Being bound excites these women.
- Being spanked during sexual intercourse with whips, belts, or other abusive-type paraphernalia is also exciting to these women. They get more excited with each slap or hit.

1. EXPERT ADVICE

A growing number of experts share the same feelings about sexual addiction and its treatment. Many believe that sex is not a "true addiction" but "only learned patterns of behavior" that are now stigmatized by our society. Researchers' reasons for their feelings are:

- Sexual addiction is the only addiction in which a person can be cured, as long as he or she uses "the drug"—that is, sex—in an appropriate way, such as within a committed relationship.
- Repeated testing has found no differences between the mental state of sex addicts and nonaddicts.
- Even though the press blows sex-related issues out of proportion, it is not listed in the *Diagnostic and Statistical Manual of Mental Disorders* because experts have not yet reached a consensus on its definition.
- Assessments of "sex addicts" tend to be subjective; the moral or religious values of the recovery group or therapist shape the diagnosis. Unfortunately for many women, reawakened values have left them feeling guilty about their urges. Some women feel their libido is just strong.

2. ESCALATING SEX DRIVE

Some women admit that they have never been in a relationship that can completely fulfill their sexual needs. Many would make love every day if they could find a man to oblige them. If intercourse or masturbation was not done, in a few days they'd be compelled to go out and look for sex. Many experts feel that unless a woman has to run to the rest room to masturbate because of a strong sex drive, nothing is wrong. They attribute this to her being more exciting in bed. Just because you want sex more than five times a week does not make you an addict.

3. PROMISCUOUS BEHAVIOR

Women who have sex with several partners in the same day or week are playing an unsafe game. Promiscuous behavior is not an indication of addiction. Women who have multiple partners without protection are risking their health. On the other hand, sleeping with several partners can be a sign of problems.

4. KINKY SEX

Rough sex is sometimes considered kinky. Some women have said that they don't need the kinky rough sex, but with the right man it's a complete turn-on. This same group of women craved to be dominated. Therapists agree that sexual behavior between consenting adults that doesn't cause serious pain or injury falls within the acceptable sex range. Kinky sex should cause concern if pain, violence, or embarrassment is evident.

5. IMPERSONAL SEX

If you sleep with someone who you'd never think about dating, much less marrying, you're considered unbalanced. Going to bed with several men who, for various reasons, aren't people you'd like to see socially falls into this category. Some women have relationships for purely physical reasons; it's considered recreational lovemaking.

6. EASY WOMEN

Some men think that a woman who orgasms easily is *easy*. Some women are so in tune with their wants, needs, and desires that it doesn't take much for them to obtain gratification. Men label these women as nymphomaniacs. So do other women. Easy women don't necessarily need clitoral stimulation, and sometimes being kissed or touched in erogenous zones is enough to send them into ecstasy. These responses don't mark them as sex addicts—only lucky.

7. TRUE ADDICTS

True addicts are rare individuals. These are people who can't stop thinking about sex even after having just made love. Yet it is rare for the woman who is rejected by the man she has just had sex with or who has been treated cruelly by this man after sex to want more sex. Women who are repeatedly driven to have sex, no matter how great the risk or humiliation, represent a tiny minority of the population, says Patrick Carnes, addiction theory's chief architect. Carnes says the addict:

- Feels "powerless" over her erotic urges, despite the risks.
- Knows deep shame and hopelessness.
- Experiences four distinctive phases during the "addictive encounter," from a trancelike state, in which an addict is intoxicated by the idea of sex, to the final phase, despair.

There are few women who fit this profile. According to Carnes, those who do have likely suffered physical, psychological, or sexual abuse as children.

A woman who feels good about herself can easily shrug off the "sex addict" stigma—even if a jealous friend or inadequate lover calls her one. A less emotional woman, a woman who is insecure, might accept the labeling. For this reason alone her addiction is harmful.

Such pressures can hurt women more than it does men. Many women still have trouble taking charge of their sexuality. Women think that being the so-called good girl will help them earn love and acceptance. The thing to remember is that no matter how often you make love, it's nobody's business but your own.

❦ *Tips on Sex*

Simple but sensitive tips to unleash and enrich passion for your lover is an excellent way to liven up romance. It's up to you whether you accept pay for passion, or whether you just like the idea of it all. Don't toy with men knowing that you aren't going to have sex with them. On the other hand, if you know that you are going to someday have the pleasures of sex with him, then a little teasing won't hurt. These tips on sex will help you instinctively get back in touch with what you already know:

1. PAY ATTENTION

Today's lifestyles have made everything so easy to obtain that we have taken for granted one of life's greatest pleasures: *sex*. Our senses have become so dull because of all the other stimuli available. Listen to this stimuli, act on it, and enjoy it.

2. CREATE MENTAL FOREPLAY

Even though physical foreplay is important in a good sexual experience, mental foreplay is just as important. Plan ahead to eliminate the not-in-the-mood syndrome. Surprise your partner with invitations to sex. Don't wait for your partner to prompt you about sex. Put it in your schedule, and don't expect him to shift mental gears whenever you get the urge. Tell him about it ahead of time. Get him excited about your next time together. He'll be so excited by the time the two of you get together he won't be able to control himself.

3. APPRECIATE YOUR BODY

The search for the perfect figure has caused a lack of self-esteem in women when it comes to their bodies. If you feel sexy, you'll look sexy. So think sexy, because a body that feels sensual is a beautiful body. You're as beautiful as you feel.

4. DON'T EXPECT PERFECTION

Make love as well as possible, but don't think that it will be perfect every time. Sometimes your best efforts will please you but not him. Give yourself an A for having good intentions. Be patient and persistent in trying to improve your sex life. It won't change overnight, but it sure will be fun practicing to become better at it.

5. DON'T LET PERFORMANCE TAKE OVER YOU

Having orgasms is an objective of sex, but it doesn't have to be the only reason or the most important one. Too much focus on performance will stop natural response. Don't think so much about sex while having sex, because it distracts from being in touch with what is really happening.

6. INCORPORATE TEAMWORK IN SEX

Both partners must cooperate to reach their full sexual potential. Working as a team will bring more sexual satisfaction than working as a single unit. In sex, you must be able to lead sometimes and follow sometimes, but it should be done in a cooperative manner because good sex is a team sport.

7. USE YOUR SENSES IN SEX

Follow your instincts and appreciate the delicate senses that help you in sex. Taste and smell are probably the most delicate subjects for lovers to talk about—and the most important when dealing with sex, especially oral sex.

Odors that are generated during sexual arousal are different for different people. Your attitude about odors will help you enjoy sex. Notice your partner's response to your touch. Be aware of how and where you liked to be touched. Revel in the sounds you make. Don't hold them in and don't be embarrassed by sighs of pleasure. Notice the changes in his breathing; this is a good indication of when he's going to have an orgasm. Tuning in to each other during sex will help sexual experiences to be better for both of you.

8. BE OPEN MINDED

Whatever you're doing now in sex is probably great, but it's not the only way to have sex. A quickie can be just as much fun as a full-scale love session. There's nothing wrong with a hurried love session in the car if you're with the person you love and care for. It's beautiful when you and your lover want sex at the same time, waiting until you're secluded behind closed doors is not always appropriate as far as timing is concerned. Having a desire for sex when your partner does is a positive in any relationship. While your satisfaction is important, you can find pleasure in contributing to your partner's satisfaction.

9. DON'T EVER NEGLECT SEX

Spontaneous or planned sex is okay. Planning helps during busy or hectic schedules. Spontaneity is great when driving home from work with your lover; if you can't wait to get home, pull over to the nearest motel and make love.

10. DON'T WORRY UNNECESSARILY

One of the dangers to a relationship is unnecessary worrying that keeps you from giving or receiving love without fear. Many women have hidden physical or emotional fears. These stand in the way of their enjoying relationships.

❦ Sexual Worries

Some of the most common sexual worries are:

1. He doesn't enjoy my lovemaking anymore.
2. Are my breasts/clitoris/vagina of normal size?
3. Is the lubrication of my vagina too much or too little?
4. I like rough sex, am I normal?
5. I have better orgasms when I masturbate, does this mean I'm a nymphomaniac?
6. I'm too fat to be loved?
7. He'd love me more if I were taller/shorter/thinner.
8. I need sex more than my partner.
9. I like anal sex, am I normal?
10. I like clitoral stimulation more than intercourse, am I normal?
11. Am I experienced enough for him?
12. This is too good to be true; it won't last.

25

Sexual Intercourse

When the big moment finally arrives, a girl has got to be ready if she's going to enjoy it. The entire basis of intercourse is to receive sexual fulfillment and to give sexual pleasure to your partner. Lovemaking varies from person to person quite considerably. If you're accustomed to a man who keeps you screaming for more, another man's strokes and variations of thrusts could be very fulfilling or very disappointing.

⚫ *Positions*

The missionary position, where the man lies on top of the woman, is the most effective position for the best sex. When a man supports his weight on his elbows in this position he has much more freedom to work his hips and body, and you can wiggle, scream, pull, bite, or wrap your legs around him with delight.

Guide his penis as he climbs on top of you so that you can help him enter your vagina. If he has foreskin, you can gently peel it back as you give him an added sensation before insertion. As he begins to enter you, make it easier by meeting him with your legs apart and your hips sucking forward to greet him at the deepest point of every stroke. You will help him as you are stimulated because his pubic bone will rub against your clitoris and deeper penetration into your vagina will be sensuously felt.

Women can control the strength of their erotic feelings during intercourse on all occasions, but many don't know this. If you want to feel him penetrate you even more deeply, all you have to do is open your legs wider and then raise them. As his penis slides with an angle it will reach farther, giving both of you more satisfaction. If you thrust upward and wrap your legs around his back as he pushes in, you may feel his penis tip touch your womb. Ummmmmmmm, this will bring pleasures that you can't resist telling your friends about. If you must talk, talk only about what you did to him, not what he did to you. You don't want any desperate and lonely women trying to get your man. Too many women are guilty of running their mouths too much.

Rotate your vagina in circles, squares, and/or alphabets at random, but don't tell him what you're doing. He'll scream out in a few minutes or so because the sensations that your rotations bring will weaken him sexually. As his penis is thrusting inward give him one of your sensuous circles and watch him twitch as you increase his pleasure. Find a common rhythm between the two of you and let the love motions flow.

Sexual intercourse and the length of time that you have sex is up to you. Suppose you would like to go on longer but your partner is about to come, here's a secret to delay his ejaculation. First, part your legs so that the pressure on his penis from your vaginal walls is lessened, and relax your vaginal muscles completely. Slow your hip movements down to a minimum and he will automatically slow down with you.

Intercourse is not supposed to be a ride on a roller coaster, starting slowly and then turning into a furious, crazy race until he comes. Women have been trained and groomed to think that the man is supposed to control the sex as well as the lovemaking sessions, but you can change that by controlling him as the two of you make love. Don't be one of the wham-bam-thank-you-ma'am crew. Start off as slowly as you like, work up an excitement of eroticism, then relax a while, change positions, get a drink or talk a while, and start again. You can do this four or five times in a love session to add variety to your pleasure. When the time comes for you to climax, try to change your position so that comfort will be the end result instead of freaky inventions of sexual positions. A woman may suffer pain through no fault of her partner just because she is in a bad or uncomfortable position at the time of climax. To enjoy the climax experience to the fullest, you must be able to feel the pleasure, not the pain of a contorted position. Besides, who wants to remember climax as a painful event. There won't be much room for joy or pleasure if you are constantly worried about pain the next time he wants to make love.

Love positions have such high levels of interest because, recently, the only way publishers could show positions was in an educational manner. Only four or five effective intercourse positions are really effective for intercourse. In these positions you won't have to worry about pain or breaking an arm or twisting your neck.

❦ The Most Effective Positions

THE WOMAN UNDERNEATH THE MAN

This position, of all the sexual positions, has the most going for it. It is by far the most basic, the most comfortable, and the most loved position of all the positions for sex. Everyone's doing it. It's the easiest position to get into. It's the easiest position to control. It's the best position, even if you have a headache that he refuses to accept. It allows both partners pelvic rotations. It is the most personal of all positions because you are actually face-to-face with your partner. It's a bit hard on a man's elbows, but he still gets just as much pleasure because he's feeling dominant. But we know that you are the one in control because you are controlling the rotations. One advantage for the woman is it doesn't require as much penetration to feel good.

THE MAN UNDERNEATH THE WOMAN

For the woman, this position is perfect. The depth that the penis will go into you is controlled. You can lean forward for less depth and penetration, or you can lean back for deeper insertion. This position allows you to pace and control the depth or the movements. If you decide that you want to squat on him, his frenum will be greatly stimulated. This is highly exciting. Men love this position but it is sometimes hard on a woman's knees.

MAN BEHIND YOU AS YOU LIE ON YOUR BACK

This position is sometimes called the scissors because of its positioning. It allows you to kiss your partner more completely as he caresses your breasts and your clitoris. Lift your legs and allow him to slide his penis into your vagina from a side angle. This unusual entry angle gives greater stimulation of the more sensitive parts of his penis, making up for the effort he has made by allowing the weight of your legs to remain on him. Your cheeks act as a buffer making it difficult for your partner to enter your vagina as deeply as he would like. The disadvantage for the male is that he has to push himself with more effort in this position for the two of you to get maximum stimulation.

EXPERIMENT

Most intercourse positions while sitting, standing, or lying down are only variations of the basic positions. Many new ways can be invented if you and your partner use your imaginations. Even so, all of these positions still don't mean as much as having good sex.

Other more exciting ways of making love can be invented if you both put in the effort. Be sure that you put some effort into your surroundings so that the atmosphere will be just as romantic as you are. Try to make him as comfortable as possible so that you can concentrate on the sensations of your vaginal contractions and palpations.

Trying every position that you have ever heard of is fun, but if your setting isn't up to par, romance won't be as symbolic as you would like.

During sexual intercourse, your man's penis will rub against the walls of your vagina. From this, sensations are increasingly pleasurable and ejaculation is the height of satisfaction. The pleasures of his penis massaging you as he stimulates the clitoris will ultimately bring you to a wonderful climax.

Just as a man experiences an erection, researchers have found that women experience an erection of the nipples while having a climax. This may not be true for all women, even if she has just experienced an earthshaking climax. It depends on the woman.

Stopping in the middle of your lovemaking is a way to take a rest or change the pace. Know whether your lover comes slowly or quickly, then adjust your vaginal gestures to fit the need. Remember that you are in control of the lovemaking; you only want him to think he is. If you are sneaking a lovemaking session and time is a factor, I say by all means hurry. But make sure that even with your hastiness, you allow some passion to seep through that is thoughtfully romantic. Otherwise take your time to make it a memorable moment.

❀ Quickies

Quickies are not always beneficial. Many men have used quick sex as a means to score or lay as many women as they can in a given amount of time. They have been as shallow as to say that they felt this was all the woman wanted or they thought she didn't need or want sexual pleasure. Quickies are the way men explained their deficiencies of not lasting longer in sex. But once you have read *Will the Real Women . . . Please Stand Up!*, you can handle these deficiencies. Most men admit that they want lovemaking to last longer than it normally does. Some men even joke about how long it does last. If lovers are lucky, however, quickies can bring lightninglike pleasures.

Opposites attract, therefore women and men are naturally responsive to each other. Nowadays likes are attracting also, especially if there are a lot of things in common. Natural responses have brought many fabulous friendships together. In a passionate embrace that usually occurs while fully clothed, a quickie could naturally occur. Raw sensuality can unfold just by watching your man untie his shoe at the end of a busy day or as he works in the garage on his old car. Some of the most common ways to enjoy quickies are:

- standing against a wall or tree
- leaning over a handy chair or table while receiving his penis from behind
- having him sit on a chair as you straddle his lap with his penis inside of you
- facing your partner while you sit on his lap or sit on his lap with your back to him

There are also several fantastic places to enjoy quickies; they are:

on a kitchen table
in a rocking chair
on a kitchen sink
on a washing machine
in a swimming pool
on a bathroom floor
by a campfire
on a chair with no arms
on top of a dryer
on a toilet seat
on a rug
in a meadow
against a closed door
under the kitchen table
on a secluded beach
in front of a lit fireplace

Quickies are beneficial because there isn't always time to enjoy a full session of lovemaking.

Ways to Enhance Quickies

- Occasionally change your location.
- Switch your usual roles.
- Wear blindfolds to bed.
- Slowly massage his erogenous zones.
- Fantasize while you're making love.
- Let your body feel every part of his body.
- Tease each other intensely.

- Set up exotic sessions for each other once a month.
- Talk openly about your sexual fantasies with one another.
- Have an orgy for two.
- Play relaxing, sensuous music.
- Meet him for lunch in a hotel.

✺ *Environments*

I believe sex can be completely enjoyed just about any place you want it to happen, but for the sake of safety, respect, legal ramifications, and relaxation, I suggest privacy and discretion. A change of pace and routine are sought-after qualities that add variety to sex lives. Variety is necessary to keep the home fires burning. Actually, the environment is the needed change to add spice to your love-making. Some favorite places as suggested by male friends are:

in the embrace of your lover's arms whenever the mood strikes
by a campfire or fireplace
on a boat (water isn't necessary)
by the lake
on a desk at the office
in a hot tub
on file cabinets
on top of a pool table
on a balcony
motel
at home
on a golf course
inside a moving elevator
in a van
on top of the car
on a friend's patio
in the guest bathroom
on a train
at the beach
on a bar stool
in a sauna

Where Not to Have Sex

• in front of children

❧

Give your bedroom a face lift, complete with new curtains, bed linens, bedspread, and scents.

❧

26

Oral Sex

Many lovers have used oral sex to reach new heights of sexual excitement. Good oral sex not only excites your partner, it will turn you on when you give it. After a few tries at oral sex, any inhibitions will soon disappear.

Many men do not know how to perform cunnilingus correctly. Long tongue strokes are a good beginning. The clitoris is the most sensitive point and it should receive the most attention. It should not be chewed, bitten, or sucked too hard. If your lover has trouble finding it, he should ask for your guidance. He should ask how you want it licked, sucked, or kissed. If he doesn't ask, then you should be woman enough to guide him in the right direction. If he still can't seem to find it, smile into his eyes as you show him. He'll appreciate your participation and openness.

Besides, neither of you will remember any embarrassing questions or moments once you lose yourself in your lovemaking. The better he gets at administering oral sex, the more orgasms you will have before intercourse begins.

❧ Edible Delights

There are three things to remember when indulging in oral sex. Some women call them the three C's.

1. Crave it.
2. Concentrate on it.
3. Continuous movement.

1. CRAVE IT

Men agree that the best oral sex they've ever had was with the women who shared the most passion. Showing love and affection for licking their penis excited them the most also. If a woman has the right attitude she has everything. Treating a man's penis like a beautiful tool of pleasure will delight him as well as excite him, therefore giving you pleasure.

2. CONCENTRATE ON IT

Being able to completely focus on your task without your mind wandering will keep the intensity high.

3. CONTINUOUS MOVEMENT

Long, continuous, and smooth movement with even strokes help keep the erotic pleasures flowing. It also keeps the juices flowing. Fast and abrupt movements have been known to decrease passion as well as the flow of love juices. Your vagina can be the central ingredient in a super dessert that can be eaten with gusto. When one lover has fears about fellatio or cunnilingus, adding variety to the sexual meal can break down barriers of inhibitions. The vagina can be coupled with many tasty delights. Placing a large towel on the bed can be used to cover your sexual areas. Surprisingly, many couples who begin with negative feelings about oral sex try it and find that it becomes part of their regular routine. It can also become a part of their nightly bedtime treat. At some point in time, your partner will want a blow job, or oral sex. This is nothing more than sucking his penis. This is not foreplay; it is a natural part of the sexual act that also includes orgasms.

As a prelude to sexual intercourse, oral sex is great and can lead to sexual intercourse. Oral sex can also be a prerequisite to sex. In most European nations, oral sex is accepted by almost everyone regardless of gender. Many women say that the United States is the blow-job champion of the world, I haven't found any statistics either to prove or disprove this statement.

Men look for women who are experienced sexually and know how to give a good blow job. Bringing your man to ecstasy with good oral sex will guide him to fulfillment and so should not be considered demeaning.

❖ Points to Remember

Some of the most significant points to remember about oral sex are:

1. Remember to kiss his penis the same way you would kiss your lover's lips. This type of kissing sensation is erotic and sensuously fulfilling to your lover because it feels as if you are making love to his dick. It sends more passionate overtures to his brain.

2. With practice and patience you will be able to take his penis into your mouth without gagging. Follow these simple steps: Use your hand as an assistant to your mouth. Start with your mouth wide enough to keep your teeth from accidentally scratching his tender penis skin. Create as much saliva as you can and suck until his penis is thoroughly lubricated. With your hand, make a tube bringing your thumb closer to your mouth. Squeeze your little finger around the bottom of his penis shaft, leaving your index finger and thumb loose. Move your hand in an up and down motion in unison with your mouth. Once you've created a tunnel of beef and you're holding it tight, open your mouth as wide as possible and relax the muscles in your throat. Compress your lips to help create pressure and watch the fireworks begin.

If you get bored your partner will know it—your rhythm will change or you'll slow down. Rest or change your momentum to something else that you'll enjoy. To inflict lasting and pleasurable torment, hold his penis shaft and playfully dart your tongue back and forth lightly over the surface of his penis head until he begs for mercy. Some men like to have the underside of their penis sucked. Concentrate on the area directly surrounding his penis hole, because this area is more sensitive to sucking.

Another enjoyable technique is to fill your mouth with hot or cold water and engulf his penis in this sensational pleasure vacuum. Sometimes his penis will be limp. But don't let it discourage you, it will soon harden. And for a nice change of pace, you can move completely away from his penis and onto his waiting balls. Men love to have their balls licked and gently sucked. For some men, their balls have to be sucked and lick-flicked before they consider their blow job complete.

Your tongue forms the most important portion of the mouth because, as a blow job perfectionist, it is your job to communicate with your partner's penis. The sides, tip, and flat surface of your tongue should be used. As a brilliant conversationalist can turn the conversation witty, philosophical, or emotional, so should you as a master of oral sex.

To accompany your mouth as a part of oral sex, there are several other elements of pleasure. Your hands are a celebrated tool also. They play an active role by stroking, holding, and firmly squeezing the shaft of his penis. Many a man likes to have his asshole probed by a finger or two while he's being sucked off. To do this effectively, feel for his anal sphincter muscle; it will help to guide your hand for depth. If he doesn't like his asshole to be played with he'll push your hand away. Don't be offended, he's just not ready for this pleasure, and he has no idea what he's missing, so be patient with him.

Other men like and prefer to have their neck, nipples, chest, stomach, arms, fingers, legs, and toes licked and sucked as a natural part of lovemaking. Go on and enjoy his entire body. Don't just concentrate on his dick. Don't be surprised if the man of your dreams never says a word or makes any noises during oral sex. He will soon become quite noisy as your technique improves. Don't get upset, just continue to tell him what you want; he'll soon oblige.

Safe sex is a guideline with oral sex also. Use a condom for oral sex, even though transmission of the AIDS virus by oral sex is still debated. If he comes in your mouth, and you didn't use a condom, your stomach acids may kill the HIV virus if it's present (see Chapter 38, "AIDS: A Women's Issue"). Otherwise it's a matter of choice as to whether you spit it out. Rinse your mouth out with a strong mouthwash if this happens during lovemaking. Some women like to use a mouthwash every time they indulge in oral sex and some use it as a common health practice whether their partners climax or not. It's a matter of personal hygiene and preference.

Lastly, remember that some men can be demanding and will try to pressure you into swallowing their come by telling you it will prove your love. This is a manipulation tactic to convince you to swallow his semen. Give him a firm *no*, and continue to be a Real Woman by not being manipulated into something you don't want.

❀ Basic Oral Sex Technique Treats

Lip, Mouth, and Tongue Techniques

When it's time for intimacy, lip, mouth, and tongue techniques can be fantastic turn ons. Eating, as many call it, is described as small sucking motions on various parts of the body. Forming the lips in a tight suction is the beginning of erotic feelings that will always be adored. Once a woman masters lip, mouth, and tongue techniques, her man will always feel loved and needed. Your lover will want you to kiss him deeply and meditatively, but give him little nippy bites on his lower lip to bring added arousal. As you lick every square inch of his body from his forehead to his toes, concentrate on giving little nips, bites, and sucks as you go. When you reach the inner side of his thighs just below his crotch you can start to nibble and lick playfully.

Nibble, Nip, Lick, Suck, and Bite

Nibbling: To nibble, you must take small, gentle, suction-type bites with your lips firmly rounded to pull the flesh of your partner within your lips. Many small and lightly forceful nibbles can bring inward pleasures to your partner. Nibble all over his body from his ears down to his ankles and watch the sparks fly. A good sensuous lover keeps her partner slightly and wonderfully off balance. During loving encounters, slow and dreamlike biting or a nibble here and there can be the sudden bright idea to set the erotic tone. Some women have had erotic success nibbling continuously on one spot with a prolonged kiss.

Nipping: Nipping is similar to nibbling with one exception, when nipping you must give little love pecks with the aid of your teeth. You should nip with care and gentleness. Your teeth are used to send deeper sensations than what would be used in nibbling. To nip your lover let your teeth, while slightly closed, slide across your partners flesh. *Do not bite*, if you are trying to nip. It should feel like you are rubbing your own tongue against the surface of your teeth. A good way to practice nipping is with a peeled banana. Trying not to remove the flesh of the banana from its stalk, use your teeth to lift any debris. The objective is not to leave any impressions on the banana as you clean it. Once you have mastered the banana you can begin to nip your partner's penis without fear of hurting him.

Licking: That is, drawing the tongue over something. There are variations to licking: long strokes, short strokes, sideways, downward, upward, and multiple tiny strokes. It's a matter of preference. Whatever it may be, vary to bring more pleasure and excitement to your partner. Practice licking on almost everything you eat. Make it fun as you do it. Don't think of it as work. From licking your own lips with small sensitive strokes to long sensuous strokes. Practice with popsicles, ice cream cones, and even sausage links to mention a few. Practice on your drinks by licking the rim without being too obvious. After a few practice sessions you'll find yourself licking your partner to ecstasy. It will become so natural and effortless that you'll do it without noticing.

Practice your licking skills daily. When you get them down to a fine art you will possess tongue manipulations that are uncontrollably erotic.

- Lick your tongue out as far as it will go and then slowly pull it back in. Do this at least twenty times a day.
- Lick your lover's lips every time you kiss him. Don't be sloppy or lazy with this one. No one wants to retrieve spit after a kiss. Kisses should be erotic, not sloppy.
- Roll your tongue up, down, in, out, and from side to side within your lover's mouth.

- Licking the roof of your lover's mouth as you kiss can spark new nerves in a relationship.
- All licks should be continuous, subtle, and smooth. No abrupt stops, always remain fluent and continuous. The best places to lick your partner are: *all over*. If you have to stop licking, remember to keep your hands moving until you begin to lick again.

Sucking: Drawing into the mouth by creating a vacuum with lips, cheeks, and tongue. Sucking is more intense than licking, but when applied correctly it may create sensations that your man will request during all lovemaking sessions. To practice your sucking techniques, try sucking on things. Everyone has the power to be a good sucker, but in order to become a great sucker you must practice often. You can suck :

- on a popsicle and try not to break the popsicle as you suck (use your tongue techniques here)
- on bananas or any other foods that desire a sucking motion.
- through straws as often as possible
- gently on your partner's tongue, in and out with slow to fast, fast to slow, long, short, and searching sucks
- your partner's nipples, gently at first, then with deeper and stronger force; pull his nipples all the way into your mouth with sucking motions

Sucking is a complete turn-on when it's done correctly. You mustn't suck too fast or too slow, but with an even rhythm to bring your partner to new heights.

Biting: When biting, use gentle bites that slightly press against the surface. Your lover will let you know if you are biting too hard, but try to learn the technique before he screams in pain. Learn to apply the correct amount of pressure on your lover so that he won't develop a negative attitude toward you during lovemaking.

❦ Oral Sex Games to Play

1. Use a cough drop the next time you decide to give him head. Suck on a cough drop for a few seconds to get the menthol working in your mouth. The warmth of your breath and the coolness from

the cough drop gives his penis a hot and cold effect all at once. It will drive him erotically crazy. You don't have to suck the entire cough drop, about ten to twelve sucks are efficient. Save the best sucking for his penis.

2. Find your favorite lip gloss or flavored taste and add some to the outer sides of your vaginal lips. Don't let him know that you've done this because it will take away from the surprise of it all. As he begins to lavish you, the added flavor will be an immediate turn on to him and he'll want to eat you until you climax. The sweetness of your new taste will drive him wild. It also adds variety to your vaginal juices and the flavors that you choose will be complementary to your sex. Buy two or three different flavors so you can change every now and then. Other suggestions are:

whipped cream
syrup
chocolate
fruit juices
powdered honey dust (I suggest Kama Sutra Honey Dust)
honey
peaches
wine / champagne / beer
powdered sugar

Be careful of anything that you put on the vagina or in the vaginal area because this delicate area is easily irritated.

3. Occasionally, you can treat his penis like a lollipop as you suck on it. Make circles around and around his penis as you go up and down on it. At the same time, caress his inner thighs, buttocks, anus, tummy, and any other parts of his body that you can reach. He'll beg for mercy.

4. Licking his testicles gently as you take them into your mouth can create sensational pleasures for him. Move your tongue up and down, from side to side, and in slow lavishing licks. This is one of the most erotic pleasures that men can experience, and not many women know this one.

5. While giving him oral sex, gently place your finger into his asshole and move it around in slow, gentle circles.

6. Hold his penis in your mouth and gently shake your head from side to side at the same time. This will send little tingles up and down his spine as well as throughout his penis.

7. Alternating your mouth with your vagina is something men love. This is called stroke dipping by women. Men tend to desire this one if the woman is open to it.

8. Have your lover get comfortable on his back. Kneel down beside him and take his penis in the palm of your hand. Run your lips slowly over his penis. Take your tongue and circle his penis head so that it simultaneously wets his penis as well as your own lips. Open your mouth and stretch your lips so that they cover the top and bottom rows of your teeth. Covering your teeth will help to avoid nicks or cutting the foreskin of the penis. The other reason to cover your teeth is to form a smooth firm ridge that creates sensations to his highly sensitive penis. As you form this smooth ridge, place his penis into your mouth down to its base and then slowly back up the head. To keep sufficient lubrication so the penis slides easily in and out of your mouth, wet it a few times with your tongue. Be aware of the speed and sensations that are the most fulfilling to him. Remember to get in tune with his body. Study what sensations make him squirm, wiggle, or yell out and then concentrate on them. He might like slow, steady, continuous in and out motions or he might prefer strong quick strokes or both. You should know what your man likes. Practice these oral manipulations on a regular basis and, before you know it, he'll be begging for more.

9. The sprinkle game is very heated up. Sucking at its very best. Sprinkle tiny suction kisses all over his body. Begin with his head and work your way down his entire body, stopping at his toes, then finally coming back up to his penis. Now slip your tongue over all the areas that you just suction kissed, circling his eyes, ears, lips. When you get to his nipples circle faster than you did before, like a whirlpool. Pull his nipple into your mouth with suction kisses, pulling as much of his entire breast into your mouth as possible. Knead his nipples and gently pull them again. Suck him with pleasure and enjoyment as if you are trying to suck for taste. Repeat these steps several times from his head to his toes.

10. The ice cream lick is one of the most sensuous of all. In this one you use your tongue to continuously circle the penis clockwise. As you slide your tongue in and out of your mouth go counterclockwise. To add more thrills and sensations as you slide his penis in and out, up and down, go slower, then faster, then slow again. The ice cream lick has very dramatic effects on your man and it is worth every minute of effort to see the results of it all. An added joy

is to put fresh whipped cream on his penis and really work him over as if you are licking and sucking on your favorite dessert.

11. Teeth make a great prop. Hold your man's penis sideways, like a piece of buttered corn. Slide your teeth up and down his shaft. Giving it a gentle little nip every now and then is fantastic head.

12. Eating fruit can be an added treat when accompanied by good oral sex. Bananas, oranges, berries, cherries, and any other luscious fruits can be eaten as an appetizer to oral sex. Rubbing the juices all over his penis and licking it off will send many sensations all over his body. Trying to keep some of the fruit in your mouth while sucking his dick is a nice addition also.

13. Mint-flavored candies, mouthwashes, or breath mints are nice to create cool sensations on his penis. A tangy tongue and mouth will cause a terrific sensation.

14. As he innocently watches TV or listens to music, unzip him and suck away to your heart's content.

15. Wake him up with the feeling of your tongue on his penis.

16. Some women feel that a loving and sexy thing to do is to lavish his penile juices after he's had his orgasm. This works well with animalistic sex. It's a fantastic topping on a sexual encounter.

17. Give him gentle kisses on his penis head in a dark restaurant. The fun of it all is sneaking to do it. Make sure the table is dressed in a floor length cloth to provide the appropriate secrecy.

18. Take your man's penis and move it gently between your lips. Hold it with your fingers while pressing its sides with your lips and teeth. Gently push his penis a little bit farther into your mouth and try to forcefully suck it in and out. Draw it in as far as it will go, pressing the end of his penis against the roof of your mouth. Suck it in deeply as if you are trying to swallow it. He'll experience the deepest ecstasy.

❧❧❧

If you do it, do it well.

❧❧❧

27

Orgasms

❖ What It Feels Like ❖

*T*here is much more to intercourse than reaching orgasm. However, women still think that good sex is reaching orgasm. Coming into "your" full sexual self will be a lot more pleasurable than being sexually who you are not. Once you learn to enjoy your sexuality, your giving and sharing will mean substantially more. Affection, excitement, and understanding will expand your sensitivity toward your desires to reach orgasm.

The what, how, and whys of orgasm are not as simple as they seem. Orgasms are the release of the tension that escalates during sexual arousal and heightened lovemaking. Orgasms are full of temperatures; temperatures of love that are hot and passionate, frigid and cold, warming or cooling. The way people achieve orgasms is reflected in the way they feel.

Sexual pleasures are strengthened by belief in yourself. During the first stages of sexual excitement, the veins in your pelvis, vulva, and clitoris dilate and fill with blood, which in turn makes your sexual area feel full and swollen. As the excitement of sexual tension rises, your body's muscles tense. You begin to breathe faster, your nipples become hard, and as he touches you, your whole body feels alive and sensitive to his touch.

Stimulation directly on or around the clitoris and slight pressure on the cervix or other sensitive areas of your body create the fullness of the pelvic area. This fullness, along with your body's arousal, builds to an exciting and wonderful peak. To reach beautiful and fulfilling orgasms you should relax and let go of all those tensions that are begging to be released. If you let go, a variety of involuntary and pleasurable contractions further increases the flow of blood to your vagina, uterus, and rectum. These are the places where waves of sensational stimulations that produce orgasms go. A female orgasm can be felt by the penis because it creates a series of strong vaginal contractions, and a woman's body will sometimes go limp.

Many women say that an orgasm feels like a sneeze, a hiccup, or a long refreshing sigh. It is experienced as slow, fast, sensuous, or intense. If a finger, dildo, penis, or vibrator is used on your clitoris or vagina, a variety of sensations can be experienced. There can also be different sensations if masturbation is done by your lover or if you do it yourself. If you have different lovers, lovemaking would naturally be different with each one and sometimes the same lover can make it feel different at different times. Orgasms also feel different as you get older or as your body changes.

❦ *Achievement*

The best and most successful ways to achieve orgasm vary with the individual. From looking at a sensuous man to touching, caressing, massaging, kissing, or deliberate teasing, licking, sucking, and penetration can bring you to orgasm. Some methods work better on some women than others, but all are a matter of personal preference.

For many women, oral sex brings orgasm faster than any other way of making love. And many women agree that it's difficult to achieve orgasm with sexual intercourse alone. Women want a multitude of sensations at once. Having sexual intercourse with clitoral stimulation, kissing, and caressing all at once usually creates an orgasm. Because of this, a woman prefers to be on top of her partner sometimes because she can control the angle of penetration as well as the clitoral stimulation.

Approximately 11 percent of all women have never had an orgasm. So if you've never felt an orgasm or you aren't reaching it, that doesn't necessarily mean that something is wrong with you or your body. Orgasms are the ultimate pleasure of sex even though sex can be enjoyed without them. Women in general can be orgasmic by masturbating because women know best what it takes to bring their orgasm on.

Just because you don't have multiple orgasms doesn't make you any less of a woman. When you begin to focus on multiple orgasms, you are getting caught up into quantity rather than quality. Don't you dare feel sexually inadequate if you don't have multiple orgasms. One orgasm per sexual act is as normal and satisfying as none or as multiple orgasms.

Orgasms are important and sex is good for a woman's disposition, complexion, and libido. Many lovers haven't come to terms with the female orgasm. Women were told to shut their eyes during sex on their wedding nights. The female orgasm became more and more complicated with every passing year. In the past, whether orgasms were clitoral or vaginal was a big controversy. Women were found to have orgasm after orgasm and this fact put men to shame with their one-gun salute. Finding real satisfaction made a big difference to women, even those who are capable of experiencing multiple orgasms found that one was not enough. A woman's lover's job is to help bring her to climax during lovemaking. Working to reach this goal will improve his technique as he practices, benefiting both of you. Insist on your orgasms so that he will know you want satisfaction. Faking can lead to dissatisfaction on the woman's part. It's like crying wolf to him, and it creates frustration and laziness. If you don't let him know he'll feel content and fall asleep without you having a climax.

❧ Helping Him to Help You

Take his hand and lead it to your clitoris; he'll get the message and start masturbating you. Help to guide his hand to your most desirable spot. Help with the rhythm of his movements by holding his hand as you show him what you like. Talk to him, and let him know what you like, for this is not the time to hold back. If you choose to have an orgasm through oral sex, tell him to lick you and rotate your hips in his face as you pull his face, nose, and mouth into your vulva. Allow his facial hair to rub against your clitoris.

After your arousal creates an orgasm, tell him what you liked the most; make it sound erotic. Wince and sigh with passion. A woman does not have to put up with unsatisfying sex from her husband or lover. Initiative on the woman's part will help the man to understand that you need an orgasm and it's his job as your lover to help you. Having simultaneous orgasms is more than satisfying, to say the least. A woman's orgasm can be triggered by her lover's sperm squirting against her cervix. Men have told me that they experience ejaculation when they feel the quivering and rippling sensations inside a woman's vagina when she comes. If you are in tune with your sensuality, you can experience orgasms easier. Don't be disappointed if you don't experience simultaneous orgasms because it isn't essential. If you don't come, you can still have fun helping your lover reach his orgasm. A common female sex problem is failure to have an orgasm. This is not unusual.

The three principal reasons for not having orgasms are easily cured if you:

- relax, and let your body feel at ease
- don't try so hard; it may elude you
- are anxious—the kind that causes a man's penis to flop

1. Relax, and let your body go limp. Some experts recommend a drink or maybe a tranquilizer to help you relax. It's a matter of personal preference. Try not to worry about climaxing. Don't tense up. Be an active participant in your sexual encounter, have fun, and think positive thoughts.

2. Don't try so hard. If your lover doesn't seem to be arousing you, manipulate his actions by having him put up a little fight for you. He can do this by holding you more, fondling, or caressing before you spread your legs for him. Give a little and decline a little; keep the session interesting and progressive. Say things to him like . . . "Kiss my ears," "Suck my breast." Take control of your sexuality by coming before him and trying to come again with him. Have multiple orgasms so that both of you will have pleasure.

3. Tolerating sex without orgasm is a matter of preference also. Many women go for years unsatisfied and unfulfilled due to lack of

orgasms. Lack of orgasms lead to the slow erosion of relationships because the frustrations surface sooner or later in detrimental ways.

A sexually happy woman is a sexually sensuous woman. She is also gratified and satisfied. Be a Real Woman and make sure you're being satisfied.

⸙

When you feel anxious, breathe deeply.

⸙

28

Games You Can Play

*H*ere are a hundred things that you can do to add spice to your relationship. A Real Woman will find ways to turn her man on even if he's not accustomed to the exotic games of love-making that you come up with. These suggestions will help you come a few months this year and maybe even the next year. You can always lengthen this list with your personal best.

1. Wake him up by licking every sensuous part of his body.
2. Massage him with honey until he can't take it any longer.
3. Ask him to teach you his favorite massage techniques.
4. Take sexy pictures of him.
5. Let him take sexy pictures of you.
6. Hide fresh cherries all over your body, then tell him to "Find the Cherry."
7. Lick him all over his body and see who gets weaker first.
8. Let him lick you all over until your heart is on fire.
9. Greet him at the door wearing heels only.
10. Serve him dinner stark naked, with you as the dessert.

11. Let him shave off all your body hair.
12. Bring home his favorite drink and play with it the next time the two of you bathe.
13. Play with his body parts as he drives you to work.
14. Be a sexual tease as he drives you to work.
15. Make passionate love before he goes to work.
16. Catch him in the shower and wash his body very slowly and sensuously.
17. Put his favorite sexy photograph of you into his wallet.
18. Make love in a tub full of water.
19. Make sexy phone calls to him.
20. Play footsie under the table at restaurants.
21. Buy him a erotic gift and ask him to be creative with it.
22. Invite a best girlfriend over and let her work as your server during a romantic dinner.
23. Buy a massager and massage him sensuously until he begs you to stop.
24. Write him erotic letters from time to time and put them in unexpected places where he's sure to find them.
25. Go on long romantic drives.
26. Buy your favorite piece of lingerie and wear it on a romantic night just for him.
27. Touch him where he least expects it. Watch his response
28. Call him at work just to say hello. Say it sensuously.
29. Sit next to him in complete silence. You can touch and cuddle, but no talking allowed.
30. Take him to a sexy movie.
31. Create your own strip show for him.
32. Meet him for lunch in nothing but your undies and a long coat.
33. Create an atmosphere of love for him. Remain playful.
34. Make up your own X-rated story in which he plays the starring role.
35. Give him a massage with oils that are sure to turn him on.
36. Have a full day of romance.
37. Tell him what you enjoy most about his style of lovemaking.
38. Give to him and accept gift from him with no expectations.
39. Put your tongue in his mouth as far as you can. Keep it neat and passionate.
40. Stay in the bed with him a little later than normal just to tell each other your dreams.

41. Plan an evening alone together, and do the wildest things that come to your minds.
42. Wear something he bought for you and nothing else the next time you are alone with him.
43. Prepare his favorite meal and give it a special name that the two of you will laugh about.
44. Next time he's too distracted to be interested in sex, dance nude for him.
45. Tie him to the bedposts for fun and have your way with him.
46. Now it is *his* turn.
47. Don't wait for him to always initiate romance.
48. Touch him as you whisper sweet nothings in his ear.
49. Nibble on his body parts during lovemaking.
50. Spend an entire evening focusing on him. Don't mention any of your problems or concerns.
51. Blindfold him and kiss him passionately. Ask him to guess the flavors that you put onto your lips. Use several different flavors.
52. Give him a day of relaxation by taking the kids and allowing him a day alone to do whatever he wants to.
53. Make love in front of a lit fireplace in the daytime.
54. Make love and then discuss each other's sensuous scents.
55. When he gets home, tell him that you've been waiting for him to come home. Then prove it.
56. Invite him to plan a romantic vacation with you. Even if it's only a day away.
57. Leave a trail of clothes for him to find you the next time he arrives home.
58. Go shopping for underwear with him, and then let him know that you don't have any on.
59. Get naked and sit quietly in front of him.
60. Lie in the middle of your dining table and tell him that dinner is served.
61. Tell him that you love the way his hands feel against your body.
62. Experiment with new positions when you make love.
63. Kiss him often and tell him passionately that you love him.
64. Play strip domino. Every time you score ten points or more, he must remove an item of clothing, your choice.
65. Have him buy his own copy of *Will the Real Women . . . Please Stand Up!*

66. While watching a movie, take his hand and show him just where to caress you.
67. As he watches you, slide a popsicle into your mouth and slowly lick it until it's gone.
68. Challenge him to make mad, passionate love to you for at least six hours in the same night.
69. Wake up in the middle of the night and hold him snuggly and lovingly.
70. Skinny dip together in the moonlight.
71. Send him flowers or a plant with a sexy note attached.
72. Have a kissing contest to see who can kiss the most passionately for the longest.
73. Leave love notes all through your home for him to find.
74. Slip a pair of your favorite panties in his briefcase.
75. Always smell your best for him. Make it a habit.
76. Keep chilled wine ready for before, during, and after love-making for sipping.
77. Ask him to strip from head to toe to his favorite song for you.
78. Shine a flashlight on various parts of his body as he dances for you in the dark.
79. Make it a habit of telling him that you love him, only if you really mean it.
80. Give good night kisses to him—make sure they are passionate. Lick the roof of his mouth from time to time while kissing. Uuuummm . . .
81. Place sexy photographs or prints in strategic and discreet locations.
82. When you know you won't be home for dinner, make a special meal and leave it in the refrigerator for him to find.
83. Wear only his favorite pair of earrings while serving him dinner from time to time.
84. Give him a sensuous foot massage, kissing his toes every now and then.
85. Lick his eyelids during lovemaking.
86. Be sure to gently suck his earlobes in between kisses.
87. Give a compliment he's never heard you give before. Be creative.
88. While waiting in line together, tell him in a low sexy voice what you plan to do to him when you get home.

89. Use your favorite scents on your bedsheets, pillows, and bedcovers.
90. Have a mold of your favorite body part made for him to keep.
91. Oil your breasts with your favorite oils and then give him a massage with your breasts.
92. Have a picnic with him in the middle of your bed.
93. Suck his bottom lip into your mouth at the end of each kiss.
94. Become a Real Woman, and remain one during sex.
95. Tell him that you are a Real Woman and mean it during sex.
96. Treat him like a Real Man.
97. Love yourself more than you love him.
98. Suck his fingers for no reason at all.
99. Write a short love story with him as the lead character and slip it in his briefcase or in with his lunch.
100. Don't forget the condoms, because good sex is always safe sex.

The point of these games is not only to give your man a good time, but also to enjoy yourself. Don't ever shortchange yourself just to accomodate your mate, because the best and sexiest times you can have are when you are both getting what you want. Being playful and remembering to have fun together is key. Playing games is not just for kids, so move down the list and be innovative, adding your own unique touch and personality to each.

❧

Keep secrets that are entrusted to you.

❧

29

The Sexually Aggressive Woman

*S*exually aggressive women make dancing look like foreplay. They gyrate their pelvises as if they were man-made. They are confident wearing low-cut clingy tops without bras. Their plan is to seduce their partners. It doesn't have to be a second date. As a matter of fact, it doesn't even have to be a date, just as long as she ends her night in erotic pleasures. Sexually aggressive women usually get what they want.

During dinner dates, it's common for the aggressive woman to touch her date on the most private places—places that aren't typical public expressions of affection. An aggressive woman doesn't exhibit normal public displays such as casually holding hands. She does things like stroking his chest between his shirt buttons or rubbing her toes against his crotch. His face exemplifies the blush that she helps create. These women are only with men who satisfy them sexually. They aren't afraid of rejection and they don't wait too long before initiating sex. They come on strong to men as early as the first phone call, and they carry condoms confidently. The sexually aggressive woman propositions men with ease and she doesn't hesitate to request things from her partner. If men aren't ready for her directness, she will dismiss them without giving them a second thought. Being by herself is not a problem because she approves of herself. Some women who are sexually aggressive are motivated by hostility toward men. They use this unhealthy aggression to subconsciously distance themselves from men, by trying to scare men away. In this is fear of abandonment and intimacy. They feel that controlling or intimidating men sexually will emasculate them until they are harmless.

But there is healthy aggression also. The female sex drive was very misunderstood until recently, and in this chapter I focus on many of the healthy as well as unhealthy aspects. The healthy sexually aggressive woman knows that she is entitled to good sex, to good sexual healing. Lust is seldom admitted by most women due to embarrassment. During my interviews with women, they talked about love, marriage, and family, but not of craving lustful sex. What I have found out from my research is that most lacked sensuality. Therefore, satisfaction was limited. Women who are healthy aggressors are fueled by their desire to control. Being the aggressor in their eyes is empowering. Having the power to get men to want them is a high, especially if they want them first. Demanding oral sex (cunnilingus) is usually a sign of the aggressor.

The healthy aggressor is not promiscuous, she just lacks inhibitions. She's a free spirit and wants multiple orgasms. She doesn't have a history of jumping from bed to bed. The aggressive woman displays her body in alluring attire that doesn't look cheap. Her behavior is straightforward. She is independent, proud to be female, and she's not sleazy. The aggressive woman doesn't play the normal male attraction games such as flinging her hair or playing hard to get.

This woman never says no when she means yes. If an aggressive woman does play by the rules, it only lasts a very short while. She relies on her ultrafeminine characteristics to attract men. Once the man that she wants is sleeping with her, she gets completely loose, fondling him, caressing his body parts, initiating sex, and introducing her sexual toys with games added. She creates enough excitement to keep from being bored. She finds ways to introduce sex into her conversation by saying things like have you read the views on orgasms in *Will the Real Women . . . Please Stand Up!* Friendly touching is a sign of availability used by this woman. She will not get overly aggressive unless she sees passion in his eyes.

✤ *Aggressive Desires*

The healthy, aggressive woman never feels the need to hide her desires. If she wants to be touched on her vagina she'll say so. Her voice and requests turn him on. Asking politely and sensuously can help to initiate other forms of pleasure. Sex is joyful and men love the unbridled passion. Going after her own pleasure is a positive attribute of the aggressive woman. Men feel less pressure when women go after their own orgasm. Putting his needs first won't make you a better lover, but pursuing personal satisfaction rates the highest when making love.

If you're afraid of rejection, play by the old rules of seduction, until romance develops. Some men are scared of take-charge women. They want the first time to be their idea, so play the game until you get what you want sexually. Some men may never reveal that a come-on by a woman makes them feel uncomfortable. Performance anxiety can set in if a woman takes the lead. A man can even lose his erection if a woman is too pushy. Remember to take it slowly until he trusts you. When you're sure he's safe, let it all loose and make safe love.

✤ *Rules for Aggressiveness*

1. Assuring your own satisfaction is not wrong or selfish.
2. Tell him politely the graphic details of what you want even if you have to read it to him from a book.
3. Don't get angry if he doesn't offer what you crave. Don't confuse table manners with bedroom manners.
4. When he touches you be sure to respond by asking for more if that's what you want.
5. Initiate sex once you sense he's comfortable.
6. Don't feel guilty when asking for more sex if you need it. He'll ask if he needs it.
7. Don't allow good loving to get too serious. Remember to keep it fun.

30

Props and Supplies

✦ Sexual Hope Chests ✦

Women should have hope chests filled with the necessary props and supplies that will help in adding variety to their sensuous lovemaking. Most of these items are probably accessible right in your home. These ideas were given to me by women I spoke with throughout my research. Feel free to vary as needed to heighten or lessen the spice. Listed here are props and supplies that every woman should have on hand to spice up your sex.

1. Flavored cough drops can be used as a stimulator toward sex. Suck on the cough drop a few minutes or so before sex. During lovemaking try blowing and sucking on your partner's body lightly as you savor the cough drop. Your hot tongue and the moisture from your mouth along with the menthol-fresh coolness from the cough drop will create a cool sensation to him. This will help your guy to keep a very nice and stiff erection. Continue this thrill until he begs for mercy. Remember to vary your moves.

2. Whipped cream can be used on all of your man's erogenous zones. Some favorite places are his nipples, stomach, navel, neck,

ears, toes, buttocks, penis, fingers, and any other hot spots that you can think of. Be careful not to get it inside the ears. This simple seduction is very inviting because you have to eat the whipped cream from your lover's body. Use slow, seductive licks to eat it off. Alternate your tongue motions by slipping and sliding your tongue in continuous lavishing licks. This one will send chills through your lover's entire body and his excitement will in turn arouse you.

3. Flavored lip gloss can be used on both sets of a woman's lips. Buy two different flavors to distinguish which will be used on which pair of lips. Every woman can't use this seductive tip because of the sensitivity of her skin. To apply this lip gloss method of seduction, spread your lips and roll on the lip gloss. The roll-on lip gloss is best for this because it glides right onto your body. This is not to alter the taste or smell but to add to it. Variety enhances!

4. Assorted lingerie is nice to wear on almost any occasion. Men won't always admit the fact that a woman in beautiful lingerie is a turn on, but watch the sparks fly when you approach him or unveil your body dressed in this beautiful attire. Make sure your bras and panties match, are clean, and are sexy when you're going to be with your lover. It adds to the sensuality of the mood.

5. Sunglasses of assorted frames and styles are glamorous when worn correctly. When wearing casual wear, wear your favorite casual sunglasses. When wearing your most glamorous attire, wear a pair of shades that fits the occasion. Every woman should have more than one pair of sunglasses to accommodate her wardrobe.

6. A man's suit is hot on a sexy, sensuous woman. A woman can wear a man's suit and add flair that invites the masculine side of the man to chill out. Women in sensuous suits turn men on in more ways than one. Accompany the suit with a low-cut blouse or no blouse at all. Accessorize with small delicate jewelry.

7. Fingernail polish adds allure and beauty to a woman's nails. Adding color to the nails sends out beautiful messages to a man, whether he's your man or not. I personally know men who won't date a woman unless she is well manicured.

8. If you'd like to have your sex and eat it, too, fruits like bananas, strawberries, cherries, and pineapple chunks are nice as an additive to pleasurable sex. Be creative as you place pieces of assorted fruit on each other's bodies.

9. Greet him at the door in nothing but an apron tied around your sensuous waist.

10. Toiletries are great for when your lover sleeps over and has

left his toiletries at home. Having a few items in his favorite brands accessible is being considerate and in tune with his needs. Keep a little basket under your counter for him with toothpaste, colognes, shaver or razor, comb, brush, aftershave. Anything you think your man might need to make his stay a little more comfortable makes him feel more connected.

11. Oils and lotions are enriching to his skin when they're readily available for a nice massage before or after sex. Men love a sensuous massage at any time.

12. Popsicles are a terrific turn-on for your lover as he watches you lick, and slowly slide the Popsicle in and out of your warm mouth again and again. Use this as a means of erotic foreplay. It works wonders. Assorted Popsicles are best.

13. Chilled wine or champagne is stimulating when poured over his body and licked off, or used for dipping pleasure. Dip his fingers into a glass of champagne and then lick it off slow and sensuous to his delight. He'll get goose bumps and you'll get turned on as you turn him on.

14. Mr. Goodbars are given as a gesture to tell him he's good. The best time to send him a giant Mr. Goodbar is the day after sensational sex. Personally deliver it to him wrapped in gift paper or in a gift box or have it delivered. No need to attach a note or send a card with it because the candy bar will say it all.

15. Fresh condoms are a necessity for every sexually active woman and man. Having fresh condoms is not only smart, but also wise. Don't expect your lover to provide this protection for you. A smart, sensuously mature woman will be responsible for her own sexual protection. Condoms also have a life span. Make sure that your condoms are not old and outdated. This has bearing on the effectiveness of your protection. Remember to use spermicide jelly with your condoms, because twice the protection is just as nice.

16. Breath mints are a handy necessity for any woman who wants to be close to her man.

17. Candles are romantic, soothing, and alluring whether alone or with your lover. When alone, candles add a special and personal atmosphere that helps you to enjoy time with yourself. They lull you to moments of subtle interludes. When with your lover, watch television by candlelight, take baths by candlelight, or just sit in the dark and talk by candlelight. Who can resist being romantic when the setting is so mellow?

18. Other lights and illuminations are nice peeking in from other

rooms. Dimly lit or colored lightbulbs add romantic overtures also. They decrease electric bills if you're living on a budget. Enjoy the magic of subtle lighting and enjoy your atmosphere.

19. Incense, potpourri, or other aromas set the mood and enhance the atmosphere. The aroma creates waves of feelings and erotic moods. It's all in your thought process, so think sexy thoughts.

20. Tape measures come in handy when playing measurement games with your lover. If he's confident in his penis size, it's fun to measure the length and width of his penis. Don't use this as a ridicule tool later on. This is only used to get a rise out of his penis and your temperature.

21. Handkerchiefs squirted with a little perfume are nice to carry in your purse or pocket. The cloth keeps the aroma of a beautiful scent on your body.

22. Costumes are a nice turn-on for men. Keep him at home by changing your look for his pleasure. Men like the idea of having more than one woman. So why don't you be that multiple person. Change your hair, clothes, and any other features from time to time to add spice to an otherwise hum-drum relationship. Dress up to look like his favorite starlet or sex goddess, or create your own look of sexiness for him. He'll be pleasantly surprised at your efforts to please him.

23. Leave love notes designed just for him everywhere he'll be. Keep them simple and personalized. Be sure to say little things in your notes that will push his erotic buttons, something that only you and he could relate to. A code or key word that the two of you use will work wonders.

24. Create your own scenes by decorating your home or apartment for a romantic trip to your favorite vacation place. If your favorite place is Rome, do as the Romans do and invent your pleasures from the scenery to the food you eat. Create a wonderful and romantic atmosphere of love for two. Stop by a travel agency and pick up brochures and travel information about your favorite vacation spot. Remember the little things like the foods, the pleasures, and the souvenirs that are found at your selected place of escape. Your lover will be surprised as well as enchanted with your thoughtfulness. The key is to escape entirely by playing the role completely.

25. Sweet additives like honey, powdered sugar, chocolate, and other delights can add tasty pleasures to your appetite. Try a few and see which ones suit your taste.

26. Balloons or flowers are fantastic when trying to make up or add cheer to your partner's day. For no reason at all send balloons or flowers and a message to let him know you are thinking of him. He'll be a little shy about it at first, but the idea of it all will send happiness and sheer delight to his brain.

27. Picnics don't have to be in the park. Why not have one for two in your living room, your backyard, on the patio, or even in your bedroom. Fireplace picnics are a favorite also. Simply prepare a picnic basket with your favorite wine and foods, then select a place to have it and indulge in the fun of it all. Have you ever had a nude picnic? Try it and don't forget to add your own spice to it.

28. Pearls are nice when worn alone. Greet him at the door in a single strand of pearls. Make sure he's the only one who gets a glimpse of you. If he can guess how many pearls are on the strand, he'll be able to choose his sexual pleasure for the day.

29. Reading to your man can be sensuous (if you can get him to sit still long enough to listen). Read a chapter or two from this book that's sure to turn him on. If he get turned on before you finish, don't worry, you can always pick up where you left off.

30. Silk scarves should touch him lightly all over his naked body. You can also use silk scarves as aprons before stripping in front of him to music.

❧❀❧

*If you want things to happen, work
to make them happen.*

❧❀❧

31

Sex Talk

❧ Conversations ❧

Conversations consist of not only what you say but how you say it. The more accomplished the conversationalist a woman is, the more she makes use of tone, facial expressions, and variation of gestures for emphasis, thought, wit, and empathy.

Sex talk is not a single exclamation of moans, groans, and squeals until finally—ejaculation. Sensuous and erotic turn-ons can be interpreted in many different ways. Sex talk is in the ears of the receiver. It creates and describes probably one of the most potent means for changing direct sex into an inviting adventure.

Noise can be associated with sex whether good, bad, pleasurable, or painful. Most women still feel inhibited or even foolish when verbal during lovemaking because of its unfemininelike characteristics. Women sometimes don't want men to recognize the fact that they are enjoying themselves.

If a woman wants to make sounds as a natural part of sexual pleasure, then she should verbally express it to her lover. As a woman becomes more aroused, her heart and breathing rates increase. As she begins to reach orgasm, these rates speed up three to four times faster than normal. No Real Woman can keep still when all that excitement is going on inside of her. Some men I interviewed were genuinely turned on by a woman's sounds of ecstasy. It made them feel the king of her night. On the other hand, some men felt that noise was a turn-off or distracting to the lovemaking. One of the most important things for a woman to remember is that she must be in tune with her own sensuality. She must discover what she enjoys in sex as she accepts her sensuality. She should also know which noise-making antics will enhance her sexual pleasures.

Exposure to sex talk can be positive, rewarding, and quite an experience if it's with a man you love and adore. The first response to sex talk is to be shocked or offended. Some women are even turned off at first. The biggest complaint by women is that they feel cheap and dirty.

Loosening up, relaxing, and going with the flow will initially seem crude and disgusting, but you'll soon find yourself being turned on by sex talk. Explicit sex talk can turn you on if you refuse to get caught up in the nice girl syndrome. As he says one thing, mentally reverse it to your positive thoughts. For example, if he says "Suck my dick, baby," then you'll say to him, "I love the way you turn me on." Then, one night when you're making love, get immersed in the sensuous thought of it all and let your private thoughts become a matter of public arousal between the two of you. After doing this a few times you won't be embarrassed to verbalize your feelings.

If you find that sex talk is not for you, then seductively verbalize your feelings by saying simple things like, "Ummmmmmm, I like that," or "Ummmm I needed that." It will give the practice you need without talking dirty. As you make love, practice verbalizing your desires and feelings so that you can communicate with your lover in an erotic way. Another good start to sex talk is to tell your lover what you want, how you want it, and whether or not it feels good during your lovemaking.

❧ Voice Tone

Nothing is more erosive than an irritating voice when making love to a man. No man wants to hear a whiny, scratchy voice when he's holding you close in the heat of passion. Many women try to improve their voices by listening to themselves on tape recorders or dictaphones. Don't sound like you have laryngitis to your lover— that can be very unsexy and unromantic. Don't spend all your time and money making yourself beautiful and then turn him off when you open your mouth. Some voice-improvement techniques are:

- Take a deep breath and hold for approximately eight seconds as you answer the phone. Let your breath out slowly as you speak. It adds to the sensuality of your voice. Continue to do this until it's natural, fluent, and pleasant.
- Soften your tone by lowering your voice every time you speak. Women with loud, boisterous voices are a turn-off. Begin now, and notice how provocative you've become.
- Practice your pronunciation and correct word usage. A beautiful speaking voice and good pronunciation are doubly seductive to any man of class. Remember, romancing your man is the goal, not discouraging him.

A good point to remember about voice quality is to think, act, and talk sensuously. Talk with sensuality and believe that you are sensuous with all your being. If you believe in sensuality you will become the sensuous person you've always wanted to be. Work on improving your voice by practicing each day. Your voice should not be abrasive or harsh. Remember also to use words that compel you to make sexy sounds when you say them.

Some words that encourage provocative sounds are words that begin with the letter *s*, such as suck, sucked, sucking, sex, sexy, sensuous, sensual, sequence, seduction, seep, and semaphore. To find more sensuous *s* words, look in the index of this book or the dictionary. They have many *s* words that can help to build your sensuous vocabulary.

Use your mouth to produce provocative sounds when you are speaking to your lover. A sweet, soft, sexy voice will lure any willing man in your direction if you are willing to put forth the needed effort. Look at it this way, men want to be needed and men need to be wanted. It's up to you as a woman to make your man feel he's needed, just as it is his responsibility to make you feel needed. Imagine all that can be accomplished when you say the right things in the right way in the correct tone to him.

❦ *Telephone Savvy*

Giving good phone sex is very important to keeping a relationship steamy. Using your imagination to make him feel good about himself helps to build his ego. Having good phone savvy keeps many men interested as well as happy. Seduce your lover by calling him on the telephone and saying erotic and sexy things. Assure him that you miss him and tell him that he won't regret your time together.

Phone sex has even become big business. Many newspapers and magazines have advertisements that feature sexy women with large breasts or male hunks with large penises encouraging you to phone in for a dollar or two per minute. They actually make you believe you're the one they've been longing to hear from. Thousands of men and women call every day for two main reasons: some want to masturbate as they listen; others want to meet women or men.

Masturbation over the phone has advantages over real life. Some obvious reasons are: you don't have to dress for the occasion and the dangers of unsafe sex are not present. Phone sex is not threatening to the listener either, because face-to-face rejection doesn't exist. There's always someone to talk to. People calling for phone sex can use their imaginations to the ultimate without embarrassment or belittlement.

Experiencing phone sex can teach you about many aspects of sex that you've never thought about before. Exaggeration is quite natural on the telephone. Even though there are professional phone sex lines, we will deal with your personal phone line and phone sex to your lover.

To make it interesting to the both of you here are some suggestions:

Your overall attitude is important. To turn your lover on with phone sex you should sound genuinely interested in the conversation. Be as verbal as you possibly can. As you talk to him, use a lot of adjectives describing yourself and your favorite sexual encounter with him. If you haven't had a sexual encounter with him yet, describe yourself and what you would like to do to him. Your description should help your man think of an image. Use your sexiest-sounding voice. Practice by using a hushed, low, sexy tone. Making sounds of climaxing will give vivid images to your partner. Coming usually lasts longer over the phone than it does in real life.

Don't fall into the trap of using the phone as a way to avoid intimacy or to avoid a real relationship. The trials and tribulations involved in knowing how to use phone sex are just for entertainment and are not a replacement for kissing, cuddling, or a real, live beating heart.

❀ *Making Sensuous Cassettes*

1. Practice on your cassette recorder to find your sexiest voice.
2. Call a phone sex line and learn the do's and don'ts of phone sex. This will help you to learn what works.
3. Remain seductive by having a gentle introduction, slow build up, and soft resolution.
4. Choose his favorite song as your background music. Make sure it relates to the two of you.
5. Choose a song that he won't sing or hum along with . . . something romantic and seductive.
6. Music should be subtle and low in the background.
7. Choose a long-playing album that makes you feel romantic and open.
8. Don't use any other provocative female sounds or moans.
9. Choose a comfortable, uninterrupted environment. Turn off the ringer on your phone.
10. Begin your tape with your sexiest hello, but don't let it sound rehearsed. Use his name or the nickname you gave him, and tell him in detail the sexy thoughts you've had about the two of you.
11. Choose sexy clothing, but take it off before taping and go naked. Taking it off heightens your romantic mood.
12. While you're thinking of him and as you begin to masturbate, tell him what you're doing as you do it.
13. Be as true and as honest as possible. Intently intensify . . . no faking.
14. Rest for at least an hour after you complete your tape.
15. The next day listen to it and if you decide to mail it to him, send it along with an erotic note. Overnight mail services are great for this.
16. Put it in his lunch box . . . or slip it into his car audiocassette deck.

Now sit back, relax, and wait for his call. Once he calls, play out one of your favorite fantasies and don't forget to sound as provocative over the phone as you did on the tape.

❦ *Noisy Turn-Ons*

Women prefer to be joyously noisy in their beds, but they have been afraid that they'll make the wrong noise, say the wrong things, and eventually turn their men off. The fact is that most men want you to be expressive and uninhibited. They don't mind if you sound provocative or expressively mellow. Basically, any sounds you make will turn your man on. Noise is an indication that your lover is turning you on, which is what most men adore. He wants to know that he's giving you what you want. Noises make him wild because most men interpret noises as kinky. They believe that they are turning you on when you make noises.

Foreign words are known to drive men wild during sex if hearing English is all they're used to. Foreign words are thought of as sensuous during sex.

Men aren't mind readers, that's why they like to be told things in bed. Telling your man that he looks good, that he smells good, or that he's good in bed are forms of sex talk that men appreciate. He also likes to be told that his eyes are gorgeous, his eyelashes turn you on, his skin feels fantastic, and other complimentary things about his body.

Another male sex talk tactic is to ask sensuous questions. A man feels desirable and important in bed when a woman whispers sweet nothings in his ear during lovemaking. Some sensuous questions might be "Can you put that inside of my vagina?" "What are you going to do to me?" "Can I taste you?" "Will you taste me?" Try to think of sex questions to ask him during lovemaking and watch him get turned on more.

You can also start off by describing what you're doing or going to do sexually to your lover. Men love this. As you move forward, put more sensuous feelings into your words. As the intensity heightens, your partner will squeal in delight and also say a few words himself!

❧ *Noise After Sex*

When it comes to sexual performance, men are basically puppy dogs who are taught only a few new tricks. After they're finished, the responses that they really want to hear is Good Boy, for the good sex. Since vocalizing is natural after sex, go ahead and sound off. Don't think about the negatives and please don't worry about it. Get in bed with your man and say what feels good to you. You'll find that the things you say will be just what he wanted to hear. Being creatures whose lives are sometimes captured by a net of words, they heighten our excitement as we perform sexually. Sex talk is a potent way of turning straightforward sex into something more erotic for men as well as for women. For many men, going to bed with a woman who has enough eroticism to talk dirty is a turn-on in itself.

Vocalizing should come natural to you, since you've been doing it ever since you were a baby. Whether it's words or just making provocative noises, it gets you back into that erotically innocent state. Don't overprepare or think too much, and for Pete's sake, don't worry. When you're with your man, let your erotic voice take over. You'll be surprised and pleased with what comes out of your mouth. You'll find that you'll know exactly what to say.

❧❧❧

Enjoy playtime.

❧❧❧

32

Turning Him On

❧ Erotica ❧

To achieve intense pleasures in sex, more sensuous contact has to be made by lovers. It can sometimes become difficult for a woman to release her inhibitions and enjoy the pleasures involved with being a woman. Turning him on as well as yourself will help you get rid of sexual hang-ups. Women feel more comfortable in their relationships as they begin to express love. Mood and privacy are the basic concerns of women when making love. Rediscover your erotica and make love more satisfying for the two of you. Some women manage to keep their sensuality in full bloom long after their friends have thrown in the towel. Staying in tune with your sensuality and your sexuality can help you to maintain heightened desire as you continue to make good love. If you've suddenly lost interest in lovemaking and you can't seem to get the hots for your lover—you have a headache, you're focused on the bills or on other nonsexual activities—you need to rediscover yourself and get turned back on. Being sexually in tune, alive, and vibrant is vital to your relationship. Women who have lost the desire or the drive to have sex are growing old before their time. Loss of

sexual appetite leads to frustrated women and the possible loss of
your man. When you suddenly lose the desire to make love or your
interest in sex, you should get in touch with your own body. If you
put out undesirable messages, the man in your life begins to think
that he is undesirable, unloved, and unwanted.

✤ Keeping Him Turned On

Here are some ways to keep your lover turned on.

1. Sit close and touch him sensuously as often as possible.
2. When standing next to him, stroke his back with one of your
   hands, remembering to move your hand slowly and sensuously.
3. When at social gatherings, brush your nipples across his
   back each time you pass him.
4. Pull him closer as you kiss him, don't let him be the aggressor all the time. He'll love it.
5. Give long, lingering, and playful kisses.
6. Make him feel that you like to kiss him by giving lots of
   tongue kisses.
7. Glide your hips toward him as you kiss him and roll onto his
   penis sensuously.
8. With all your clothes on, straddle him and kiss him passionately.
9. Play with his nipples each time you kiss him.
10. Do all the things he likes.
11. Blindfold him and make love to him. Tell him no peeking.
12. Blindfold him and give him head for at least an hour.
13. Become willing to share your sensuous ideas with him.
14. Look directly into his eyes as you jack him off.
15. Look directly into his eyes as you masturbate yourself.
16. Prepare his favorite meal, and name a new dessert after his
    penis.
17. Excuse yourself from his presence, insert your forefinger into
    your vagina, return to him, and as you hug him give him a
    long sensuous kiss. Then slowly glide your scented finger se-
    ductively under his nose.
18. As you stare into his eyes, slowly and seductively suck on an
    ice cube. Move the ice cube in and out of your mouth with

your tongue. As you release it from your sensuous lips, lick the rim of your glass slowly and sensuously.

19. Have him massage your clitoris with his penis as a part of foreplay.
20. Wear something sexy to bed at least five days out of the week.
21. Buy a garter belt and wear it on special occasions.
22. Buy sexy lingerie. Indulge in this sensuous pleasure and he will, too.
23. Buy sheer stockings instead of support hose.
24. Wear lace bras regularly.
25. Read sexy books to liven up your sensuous thinking.
26. Give good phone sex. Say sweet nothings on the phone and don't forget to coo and ahh a lot. Seduce your man by making a sensuous call to him for a date.
27. Hire him for an evening of passionate sex. Tell him that you're going to pay him a hundred dollars an hour. He'll be thinking about it all day.
28. Look good when your man gets home from work. He probably sees beautiful women daily, some probably flirt with him. Don't give him a reason to have an affair.
29. Tell him that he turns you on and mean it.
30. Be a good listener when he talks to you, look directly into his eyes and listen to what he has to say.
31. See it in your heart to give him his fantasy.
32. Work to be the best sex partner he's ever had.
33. Think about sex with your lover on a regular basis. The more you think about it, the sexier you'll become.
34. Schedule two fantasy dates per month. He's responsible for one and you're responsible for the other. Keep all plans secret from each other. Plan an evening around the fantasy. It can be as wild as you want. The trick is to make it a date to remember.
35. While performing oral sex take a piece of ice into your mouth. As you begin to slowly lick him, rotate the ice cube all around his penis. Be sure to suck, lick, and massage him with your iced tongue until he begs you to stop. This technique is very beneficial to a limp penis or one that has gone to sleep before its time.
36. Flirt with him on a regular basis. Use your body while flirting. Send erotic, yet silent flirtatious messages to your partner while in a crowed room of people.

37. Tie your lover to the bed and tease him over and over again. The active lover waits until the passive lover is tied up before she takes her clothes off. Once she ties him up, she seduces him with her actions. She touches him with parts of her body only. After seductively stripping for him, kiss him all over his body, remembering not to miss a single spot. Alternate soft to firm touches on his body. This will naturally drive him wild. As he squirms and twitches about, leave him there and get a drink or find something else to do for about two minutes. These two minutes that you're away will feel like twenty to him. Once you get back, start the process over again, beginning with light kisses all over his body.

38. Send items of clothing to your lover. Send him one piece at a time on a weekly basis. You can take as long or as short a time as you want to send him clothes. For example, if you want him to receive all items in one week, send everything at once. If you want the time to spread out over two weeks, send half this week and half the following week. If you want to drag it out longer, select the order that you want to send the pieces of clothing and stretch it out until you're ready to be fitted by your lover. This game can be as sensuous and erotic as you want it to be, or as subtle as you want. These pieces of clothing should be sensuous and erotic. Once he's received a complete outfit allow him to dress you so that later that evening he'll be able to also undress you.

❧

*Make up your own games if you don't
like the games other people play.*

❦

33

Signs of a Sexual Dud

*I*f a woman pays attention to the cues, she'll possibly be able to spot a sexual dud before she wastes her time. Sexual duds give off very clear signals that women can read very easily. These men are narcissistic and self-centered from the very beginning. Many women ignore the obvious signs because he either makes her feel like he's Mr. Right or he brags about his sexual abilities or conquests. Some of the usual signs to watch for are:

- Sexual duds ignore the fact that they are duds because they are so busy trying to prove themselves to a woman that they ignore their inabilities.
- He builds himself up verbally to compensate for his lack of sexual prowess.
- He cannot be measured in inches and he is often overbearing and demanding.
- He will always order dinner for the two of you, he won't let you drive your car, and he's obviously accustomed to controlling his lovers.

- His bedroom manners will reflect his personality, so watch for tacky signs.
- Men who are driven to perform athletically will usually have less left for lovemaking.
- Some men put so much energy into sports because they are trying to compensate for their poor performance in sex.

❖ Sexually Dull Types

1. HE'S TOO SERIOUS

He's perfect in his opinion, but the world and everything else in it is not. He verbally curses all automobile drivers. He's critical of restaurant food and your taste. This guy will not cuddle or give affection.

2. YOU'RE JUST MY TYPE

If he tells you that you're just his type . . . watch out. The woman he's with is his measure of being a man. Women are sexual objects in his eyes.

3. THE UNSAFE MAN

He doesn't talk about safe sex and is irresponsible about contraception. He's concerned only with his own fulfillment.

4. THE UNFULFILLED MAN

He has low self-esteem and constantly talks of his bad luck. He feels powerless and useless. He expects everything to be a letdown and he's probably right.

34

Your Bedroom Excitement

What it takes for women to add excitement to their bedrooms is the focus of this chapter. Breasts and buttocks are not the keys to being excited in bed. You've got to possess the erotic qualities that drive men crazy in bed. Many women think it's their face, smile, or even their bubbling sense of humor. But it's much more than any of these outward qualities. It's an extra ingredient that women possess that they can't quite explain.

Women who possess this ingredient will have men risking their careers, marriages, and financial statements. Any woman who wants to be the woman who can drive men to ecstasy can become the mistress (or the wife who acts like the mistress) by developing a new mental attitude. Details on possessing qualities that will raise your level of lovemaking are covered in this chapter. You will be considered a perfect lover by your mate after this erotic makeover.

Sexual techniques, exercises, diet, psychology, and understanding will add to the sex life you already possess. It will develop into an event of more erotic stimulation with pulsating, earthshaking, and successful adventures of love.

My experiences are purely personal and simply editorial. I have served on no dynamic sex committees nor written for leading sex magazines, but I have spent some time on top of my lover. My experiences have also taught me to chart my erogenous zones and document my personal experiences. I have had conferences with strangers, friends, moms, coworkers, dads, and psychologists.

Understand that sex is not a manipulative adventure; it is a way to release tension and express love. Erotic women love men, sex, and sensuality. Women should not be afraid to enjoy the pleasures that are brought to their bedrooms. Being able to give your man pleasure after you've read this chapter will make him love you even more.

Many women enter into sex without knowledge of where the penis is actually supposed to penetrate. My goal is to help mature, capable women fulfill their personal needs first, then to help them into fulfilling their man's sexual needs.

Being unaware of what to do when faced with real-life sexual encounters that are positive, healthy, and wanted has been a dilemma of many women. To add confidence to your bedroom excitement, I will show you how to:

> use bedroom tactics that work
> help him keep an erection
> please him orally
> accept your sexuality in a positive way
> turn a man on and keep him turned on—in bed as well as out of bed
> communicate with him before going to bed with him
> know what you're supposed to know
> increase female independence

Potential sexual pleasures are within the reach of women and they have a right to enjoy these unleashed pleasures. You can train yourself to be a perfect lover. Erotic pleasures belong to you. With the knowledge and training you can be far from a slave to men.

To become more exciting in bed, you must cater to your man's fantasies. In achieving erotic pleasures, a woman must do three things:

1. She must understand her own erotic potential and how to exploit it in a positive way with her lover.

2. She must know what her man wants most from her in bed and how to give it to him.
3. She must know how to go about getting and keeping the man she wants.

These points are all important, but the last one is the most important, because not every woman has a man waiting in her bed. In fact, finding an exciting bed partner you want can be the most difficult part of the whole sexual exercise. Nothing is worse than being caught in a sexual relationship that has no spark. Exciting sex isn't something we inherit. Training and counseling are essential even though it is physically and psychologically complex and in many cases affects our entire being. Every woman needs training that will equip her with the information to satisfy her lover, and will also give her the necessary means and understanding to use that information in a positive way.

Here are some suggestions to help you learn to pay closer attention to your relationship. Some of them sound like simple housework, but each task can involve him more deeply as you add sexual excitement to your bedroom.

1. Plan regular activities that involve the two of you. It might be sexual or nonsexual, anything that creates exciting rituals for the both of you.
2. Rent a romantic movie and then try to top the love scenes.
3. Plan your next vacation together and make sure it's a romantic getaway instead of visiting relatives.
4. Organize and plan dinners for two that are romantic and alluring. You should not invite the kids to these.
5. Keep track of social events and plan to spend happy times together.

❦ Bedroom Manners

I have a checklist that covers the essentials. Some important things that women should remember about bedtime manners are:

• The owner of the bed delegates who will sleep on which side.
• Try to wear something sexy to bed at least three hundred times in a year.

- Provide toiletries for your partner such as towels, a toothbrush.
- Show him where the light switches are before retiring.
- Don't make unnecessary noise while he's sleeping.
- Don't leave your bedtime gear at his place unless he asks.
- Never take for granted that he'll be back the next week.
- Bring extra underwear if you sleep over. Putting on the same underwear after sex isn't very sexy.
- Don't have excessive toiletries lying about, or he'll think he's in a heavily trafficked area.

Moving your personal items to his place without notice is very inconsiderate. If he wants to snuggle and you don't, *compromise* and do a little of both. If he snores, don't get angry, move to another location, but leave a little sexy note telling him where you are. End it with "Send ransom."

❀ Bedroom Myths

There are many myths that circulate about the bedroom. These are no more realistic than any others. The myths stop here.

1. SEX DRAINS YOUR ENERGY

On the contrary, an energized love session can actually revitalize you. Some female athletes feel their timing is much better when they've had good sex.

2. TO LOOSEN UP OR RELIEVE TENSION, HAVE SEX

You would actually benefit more by having sex. It aids in normal fatigue that comes from hectic schedules. So go ahead and treat yourself to good, relaxing sex.

3. HAVING SEX MORE MAKES YOU WANT MORE

This is absolutely true. It's a life cycle. Even though studies are being done on this subject, one thing is for sure: hormones released with sexual activity increase sexual desire. Sex causes women to feel energized, restful, and sometimes slightly intoxicated, therefore creating a desire to have more sex.

4. SEMEN IMPROVES YOUR COMPLEXION

According to Dr. John Ramono, an attending dermatologist at New York Hospital–Cornell Medical Center, vitamins need a cofactor to be absorbed through the intestines and cannot be absorbed through the skin. Therefore, semen does not nourish the skin or prevent wrinkles as some people think. Semen is high in fructose, a form of sugar, therefore as a topical skin treatment it would be unhealthy.

5. SEX IS THE BEST WAY TO LOSE WEIGHT

This is true if you skip meals and make love every twelve hours. If not, forget it. No one has been able to give accurate counts on calories burned during lovemaking. The most popular estimates are:

foreplay: 100 calories an hour
intercourse: 100 calories an hour
orgasm: 400 calories an hour

Orgasm may sound like a dream come true to dieters, but most orgasms last only three to fifteen seconds. That's 1.6 calories at most per seismic event. The grand total is 201.6 calories for two hours and fifteen seconds.

6. THE BEST LOVERS ARE PHYSICALLY FIT

Being physically fit helps the body to work better, but it does not determine the worst or the best in a woman. Some women feel that being in shape helps them to make love better. Physically fit bodies in the bedroom are gaining popular attention. Women out of shape tend to tire faster. Women who are in shape experience more powerful orgasms along with more forceful pelvic contractions. Being physically fit may not cure sexual problems, but it will definitely elevate the mood.

7. Flat-Chested Women Have Strong Sex Drives

Some do, some don't. Breast size has absolutely nothing to do with a woman's sex drive. Some women are stimulated by breast play, and to them the breast is extremely erotic. This doesn't matter whether breasts are big or small.

8. Birth Control Pills Increase Sex Drive

Some women are more relaxed once they begin taking the pill. They feel freer to let go and really enjoy sex.

9. Masturbation Causes Blindness

Masturbation is natural, healthy, and in some cases therapeutic to preorgasmic women. William Masters, M.D., of the Masters & Johnson Institute in St. Louis estimates that 90 percent of all men and 85 percent of all women in the civilized world masturbate. Modern sexologists assure us that although self-manipulation is not responsible for creating heaven and earth, it never hurt anyone either.

10. Every Orgasm Feels the Same

Orgasms come in a variety of feelings, from mild to industrial strength. The intensity of the orgasms depends on various things, such as time of day, mood, time of month. Orgasm myths can cause unnecessary worry for both men and women. Women sometimes feel quiet orgasms that are sometimes just as pleasurable, says sex therapist Betti Krukofsky. A man likes to see women climax noisily to feel his macho pride. If she's quiet he feels he's failed.

11. WOMEN DON'T NEED TO ALWAYS CLIMAX DURING SEX

If a woman doesn't climax, the blood that fills the labia takes a while to dissipate and she may be left with an uncomfortable throbbing and bloated feeling. Women don't need to have an orgasm, but they feel much better when they do.

12. MARRIED COUPLES HAVE SEX AT LEAST TWO OR THREE TIMES A WEEK

Couples in their twenties tend to have sex every day; thirty-to-forty-year-olds have intercourse between two and three times a week; forty-to-fifty-year-olds once a week; and sixty plus less than once a week. A couple can have sex twenty times a week, once a week, or only on holidays. A problem exists if one partner wants sex more than the other.

13. MARIJUANA IMPROVES SEX DRIVE

Smoking marijuana will not make your beloved more attractive to you, cure sexual hang-ups, or make him more imaginative in bed. Marijuana might put you in the mood and it might heighten your pleasure. Marijuana smokers tend to believe their orgasms are more intense, but what is really happening is that the heart rate is speeding up to 240 beats each minute. This drug also induces an obsessive state of mind. Getting high distorts your perception of time, making you think sex is lasting much longer than it really is.

14. SEX LENGTHENS LIFE

Aging does not mean the end of lovemaking, but information abounds on sex and the older man. His erection is not as rigid and more direct stimulation is required to attain an erection. Frequency of lovemaking is not linked to longevity. Sex does make you want to live longer, says William Masters.

❈

*Do something each day that makes
you feel good about being alive.*

❈

35

Things Women Fear in Bed

*F*ear blocks pleasure. If you are focusing on your personal faults when you should be focusing on lovemaking, you may be cheating yourself of one of life's greatest pleasures. Emotions are complicated and so is the list of anxieties that are taken to the bedroom. Most women are ashamed of their sexual fears, so they try to hide them from the men in their lives. Anxiety and secrecy reinforce one another. Embarrassment is certainly the key to the number one female question.

✥ Body Image

Insecurity about a woman's body is a cover for a deeper sense of sexual shame, a fear that there is something unattractive about her body whether it be odor or genitals. Work to challenge old beliefs so that you can enjoy full sexual pleasure as an adult. Exploring your own feelings can release old baggage that you might be carrying around. Self-consciousness about the body is only one item in the catalog of common sexual fears.

❀ Loss of Erection

When the man suddenly begins to lose his erection during the heat of passion, most women blame themselves. The fact is, women are left in the cold on the subject because men just don't want to talk about their impotence. They are too fearful or embarrassed. Most women consider a man's ability or inability to have an erection to be a direct measure of her desirability. Women are known to take the responsibility for the success of maintaining relationships. When men are having problems, women are expected to automatically fix the problem.

Asking questions instead of giving up on love can end many unexplained fears in a relationship that's gone cold. Sexual communication can calm, reduce, and sometimes diminish fears about a man's sexual performance. People freeze up on conversations when they most need to talk. Communication holds the key to reducing sexual problems.

❀ Pregnancy

Even intelligent and mature women take chances, say gynecologists. More and more women are becoming fearful that they won't be able to become pregnant when they want to. These women try to get pregnant just to prove to themselves that they can. If a woman in the "want to" group doesn't get pregnant without protection, then she begins to second guess her ability to conceive. This source of tension and wondering creates questions like "Have I waited too long?" or "Can I afford to wait any longer?"

Taking chances without protection loads lovemaking with anxieties. It's much wiser to work out ambivalence about pregnancy by thinking or talking things over instead of scaring yourself each month by taking unnecessary chances with your body.

✤ *Oral Sex*

Many women fear that they don't know what they are doing when it comes to oral sex. They're afraid they may bite their lover's penis or that they may gag. Some women are afraid to receive oral sex because they are ashamed of their genitals and can't believe a man would enjoy kissing or licking them. There is a tremendous amount of guilt and shame attached to oral sex. Even though many men are eager to perform it, many women are still quite ashamed to have it done to them. If you are ashamed to have it done, tell him. And remember that he probably would not volunteer to do it if he didn't get pleasure from doing it.

✤ *Growing Older*

Many women worry about losing their sex appeal as they enter their thirties. From the tiny lines in her face, to the fact that her body tone is becoming more difficult to keep, causes a woman to worry. Sex is usually a very important part of a woman's life. The claim that women don't reach their sexual peak until their forties is hard to believe. Experts say that it's true and studies confirm that women enjoy sex more as they gain experience and control in their lives. Traditional attitudes have caused women to think less of their sexual appetites. Our mothers lived restricted sex lives and they looked much older at our age than we do. Fear of expressing sexual wants and desires have helped to age our parents because of all the stipulations and anxieties on sexual freedoms. Taking on younger lovers used to be condemned; now it's a natural part of the lifestyle of a sexually aggressive and free woman. The major fears women have had are due to rules set by men on what women should and can be sexually. The truth is, many men just can't keep pace sexually with women.

❦

Let things happen naturally.

❦

36

Love

Romance is thought to be made in heaven, but real love often begins long after sexual passions have cooled and fantasies have ended. A woman must give herself to lovemaking with real enthusiasm. Love is the sharing of self that makes a woman whole. Love gives a woman her existence and a sense of purpose. Women who respect love and revel in love should learn to understand it. You can enjoy life and yourself without love and be physically satisfied, but only with love can you be fulfilled. Imagine that you are in a relationship that's full of hope and positive vibes. You feel good about yourself with this person. Your self-esteem is high, you're having fun, you feel the heat when you're with him and you enjoy the intimacy. Just the two of you, and love.

❀ *Falling in Love*

Many significant factors contribute to falling in love. Though these factors vary in numbers as well as in levels of emotion, women have told me their ways of knowing when they're in love.

You are in love when :

- you think his childish ways are endearing.
- your ways have become more spiritual, generous, and sympathetic.
- you begin to buy lacy lingerie to show your stuff.
- you begin to subscribe to sports magazines just for him.
- you adjust to his lifestyles.
- you begin to use the word *we* more.
- you send love letters for no reason at all.
- you listen to every word in love songs.
- you spend an afternoon of golf—following him instead of playing.
- you only call your friends when he's out of town.
- you begin to forget your priorities.
- you get rid of old gifts from old lovers.
- you forget to eat because you thought of him.
- you lose weight without trying.
- you allow him to choose your new hair style.
- you wear a dress you hate just because he bought it.
- you feel that he can do no wrong.
- you stop fantasizing about other men.
- you think he's adorable when he buys you tools for your birthday.
- you blame your girlfriend when he flirts with her.
- you keep score during his favorite football game.
- you give up sweets.
- you live in and out of your car due to stayovers.
- you think his bald head is sexy.
- you forget he's bald-headed.
- you think his sweat smells sexy.
- you shave under your arms and legs daily.
- you try to kiss up to his mother even when you dislike her.
- you give him pet names or nicknames.
- you see him and your temperature rises.
- you feel his touch and your body tingles all over.
- you see someone who looks like him and your heart begins to flutter.
- you call his mother for no reason at all.

- you forget that he's a slob.
- you ignore the fact that he snores in bed.
- you think he's exciting while he sleeps.
- you laugh at his dull jokes.
- you forgive him for screwing up.
- you buy his Christmas gift in June.
- you let him drive your car even though he won't let you drive his.
- you try to please him too often.
- you compete against his ex-girlfriend or ex-wife.
- you massage his feet even though he has athlete's foot.
- you kiss him even though his breath stinks.
- you don't notice the large fluid-filled bumps on his face.
- you rearrange your closets and drawers to make room for him.
- you tell all your close friends not to call even when you are doing nothing special.
- you are more happy with him than you are with anyone else.
- you respect his opinion.
- you suck in your stomach when he's around so that he won't notice your fat.
- you think that his animal mannerisms are sexy.
- you are able to help him become even a better lover.
- you no longer crave your favorite foods, you crave his.
- you don't take a bath right away after sex, because you want his scent to linger a little longer on you.
- you try to keep your panties that are your period panties hidden so that he won't think you're a slob.
- you ignore the fact that his feet stink.
- you put love notes in his lunch box.
- you'd rather hear the truth, no matter how painful.
- you are open to discussing your religious differences.
- you think he's too helpless to shop for groceries.
- you find him attractive, pot-belly and all.

❦ Obsessive Love

In the beginning, it's not always obvious that a relationship will become troubled and painful. Many couples say that initially their relationship was the source of great happiness, and they recall the lusty, glorious sex they enjoyed. They recall the best friend syndrome that they felt when talking to their partners. Sex was an unexplainable high. With very sexual and constant approaches to lovemaking, a relationship that, at first, seemed to have high hopes can soon turn frustrating and painful.

Women who experienced obsessive love felt as though they had lost total control of their lives. The relationships that became obsessive usually ended with great difficulty and sorrow. It's a story many women are familiar with. As these women broke free from these obsessive relationships, they began to help themselves as well as others.

Some of the aspects of obsessive love that women have had to deal with are:

- wasting years of their lives with men who didn't care for them
- traveling the long, hard, and strenuous road to recovery
- having frustrated long-term affairs with married men
- experiencing emotional or physical abuse

Over the years, women have shown courage in finally breaking free of obsessive love. Writing down details of their pain is an avenue to healing. Obsessive love rarely ends happily, but it's noted for identifying symptoms of destructive relationships and about healing from the stress and pain of obsessive love.

❧ *An Obsessive Picture*

Not every woman experienced her relationship as satisfying and fulfilling at the beginning. Many women say that they experienced trouble from the very start. They felt frustrated, sad, and yearned for a fulfilling relationship. They became so hooked that they could not stop thinking of the man. In the midst of these affairs they were drained of energy and their lives became difficult. The obsessive relationship became critical and very insulting and self-esteem dipped to an all-time low. Women also felt that it was their duty to make the relationship work (see Chapter 35, "Things Women Fear in Bed"). Many lovers were so attached that they couldn't walk away from the pain they were experiencing. This same group felt that the man needed her to survive. Waiting and hoping to see a change in him kept many holding on. They said that their lovers would give enough attention to let them know that he was interested. However, he would be so inconsistent that hopes would shatter.

When a goal is too easy or too difficult we tend to give up. When small, positive feedback is present, we stay to fight. We may not be getting enough from it, yet we stay. Some women say that they went to great lengths to avoid this obsessive love, but somehow he would always find her. Some women said that they felt completely different, uninhibited and satisfied, when they were with him. He made them feel sensuous and sexy.

✦ Dark Obsession

For the woman who was not capable of respectful relationships, the continuous pain of love and the inability to end the relationship for good, brought emotional, and sometimes physical, abuse. Women in these relationships are not only beaten, but they are beaters as well. If they are on drugs and their addiction escalates, so does the violence and abuse. While experiencing these dark obsessions, if a woman felt that her man didn't care, she might try suicide and then call him to tell him about it.

✦ Breaking the Cycle

It is not easy to leave a painful relationship, but it is possible if the person is ready and/or gets help. Powerful inner strength was reported to be found. Many also found undying strength in religion. Women who had experienced obsessive love found that breaking free was an uphill struggle. For some women, trying to forget him was more difficult than they thought possible. Physical separation was not enough.

Many women suggested innovative ways to help get over an obsessive love. Some women found help from their churches, where they regained their self-esteem. Other women visited close friends to regain identity. After all the trying and waiting on their men to change, many women finally realized that the men could never give them what they wanted. Many women benefited from counseling and using a twelve-step program. They began to understand and learn from their mistakes. Learning how not to repeat these mistakes was a major challenge. One of the books that I found to be a great help to women was *Women Who Love Too Much* by Robin Norwood. If an unhappy affair has you by the throat and you still want it, you are a victim of obsessive love. These are some tips to help you soften the blow until you can get help.

1. Give yourself some space. When you're in an abusive relationship, you usually stop voicing your own opinions and begin to deny your needs. You then begin to doubt your ability to see the situation clearly.

2. Trust yourself. After you make a clear decision, trust your judgment. Making some wrong turns can later help you to make the right decisions. The key is to trust yourself. Believing that you can and will make the right decisions will help you to move forward.

3. Set small goals. Finding a better life often requires planning. Make a wish list naming everything you want. List long- and short-term goals. Decide what steps you need to take to reach your goals. Break each goal into steps so they are manageable. Work toward them day by day.

4. Figure out why you loved. Make a list of all the traits that you want in a lover. What you'll end up with is your missing self, the person who you wish you could be. In an addictive state, you'll forget the person within you. Our love affairs offer potential to grow personally.

5. Uncover the real issues. When you're depressed over a troubled love affair, it helps to step away from the experience and take a look at your life. To examine what is going on in the present, both the good and bad, will help you to see a clearer picture. Ask yourself what makes you satisfied and happy versus uncomfortable and unhappy. Write it out as a list. Examine your past the same way. Writing about your life is an invaluable tool for understanding the patterns in your struggles with yourself and others. Many feel that insight was gained from their relationships. This, in the long run, helped in their personal growth. Many women felt that their experiences have helped them in both good and bad ways. Thus, new insights, awareness, and a greater inner strength and

confidence were developed. Many moved on from their obsessive relationships to enjoy healthy, stable, and satisfying relationships with their men.

❧ Lasting Love: Keeping Love Alive

Lasting love takes two. While nothing lasts forever, there are certain things that women can do to help their love remain strong and be fun. Women who have been in relationships for five years or more were interviewed for this section. What I realized as we talked was that it was not the quantity of gifts, money, or material items that helped their relationships survive, it was lessons learned together.

❧ Beautiful Lessons to Remember

1. PERFORM RITUALS OF LOVE

Rituals are necessary to keep love alive and interesting. Here are some common love rituals.

- Help keep each other safe, secure, and warm at all times.
- If one of you takes a briefcase to work, the other writes a love note and slips it in the briefcase.
- If one of you goes away overnight, he or she leaves a love note on the pillow.
- If one has to work on a Sunday, the other brings the newspaper, goes along for company, and remains quiet.
- Even if busy, the other stops to call during the day.
- Hold onto each other for one minute without a sound at various times of the day—mornings, evenings, when nervous, when company leaves.
- If watching television, stop for a moment to hug the other one.
- Sleep together and curl up together like spoons.
- Allow and give regular touching.
- The one who is angry makes up by telling a "Once Upon a Time Story."

2. TELL HIM HOW WONDERFUL HE IS

Tell him how much you love him, how happy he makes you, how much you enjoy spending time with him. Get in the habit of stroking his ego and do it regularly and for no reason at all. Try to love the part of him that is the least perfect and before you know it you will.

3. MARRY YOUR BEST FRIEND

No matter how old the relationship or the marriage is, continue to talk with one another. A man can be your best friend if you give him half a chance, but many women feel that men are looking for passion instead of friendship. It's said that there is nothing more passionate than friendship. As fast as the world is moving and changing, there are many things to talk about. If you marry your best friend, the talk never grows old, the sex never grows old.

4. NEVER PURPOSELY HURT FEELINGS

Learn to express your frustrations and voice your anger without aiming for the jugular. Cruel words can't be taken back or forgotten. Be careful because strength can't be gained by lashing out with unkind words. Whatever you say harsh will work on both of you because it takes both of you to keep this boat afloat.

5. KEEP YOUR INTIMACY A MYSTERY

Closeness enriches your marriage. To attain intimacy in your lives here are a few suggestions:

- Learn to enjoy each other's togetherness, even when doing different things.
- Wake up early enough to allow time for horseplay and breakfast together.
- Wake each other up for good-bye kisses when going away on business trips or out of town.

- Respect each other: try wearing clothes and scents that both of you like.
- Continue to play games and court one another.
- Cherish your times in solitude together. Revel in your privacy.

6. REMEMBER TO KEEP THE PASSION BURNING

If you want to keep your love alive, you won't wait around for sudden moods of passion to strike. Great sex needs play, which is different from traditional foreplay. Playing stimulates your sexual appetite. By playing you can set the stage for preplanned lovemaking later. Make your own magic; don't wait for it to come to you.

❧ *Reasons to Make Love*

If you're finding it a problem to make love to your man, stop making excuses and find the reason why! Has it been weeks, months, or maybe even years? Okay, you're a little busy with the kids, the job, your own career or just overextended on just about everything. So what? Putting sex last is a little selfish on your part. Oh, you say you've forgotten how to have sex—so it's been that long. To make love tonight or any night should be fun, so to help you out I've listed some reasons to help make it fun.

Reason #1 You want to make love: Making love at anytime for more than thirty minutes will help to burn off those calories that you're struggling to get rid of.

Reason #2 Breakfast snack: For that early morning love session . . . rename it breakfast. Everytime he asks for breakfast, give him sex. Tell him having him for breakfast makes you hungry for him.

Reason #3 Brunch: For that middle of the day love session . . . rename it brunch. As a light snack, give him head until he comes.

Reason #4 Dinner: For a late night love feast . . . call it a late night snack and have him eat *you* until *you* come.

Reason #5   Your dinner date was canceled: Have him get dressed to go out, but serve him a romantic dinner for two at home with candlelight and the whole bit. Then strip off his clothing and make love on the kitchen table.

Reason #6   You'd like to play sex tennis: Reserve a day to play tennis and tell him that the only balls you'll need are his. Then cancel the game and make wild, passionate love.

Reason #7   You have a special gift for him: Tell him that you have something special for him and give him only two guesses to figure out what it is. If he doesn't guess what it is, he has to give you head. If he does guess it, you have to give him head.

Reason #8   You want to feel the fire: Gasping, panting, and screaming are required in this reason to make love. Besides it won't hurt the sound system.

Reason #9   You need practice: Tell him that you've found this new game to play and the more you practice the better you'll get at it. He'll want to play more often if you use your imagination in the bedroom.

Reason #10   You need sleep: Have a wild, passionate love session to sleep more peacefully. He'll understand after you tell him why it's his duty to help you go to sleep. Afterward, fall asleep in his arms.

Reason #11   There's nothing sensuous showing at the movies: Tell him that you'd like to make your own movie with him as the star, even though we already know he's just the costar.

Reason #12   You want to give him a sensuous back rub: As you sensuously rub his back, slide your breasts, buttocks, and vagina all over his body. The stimulation from the heat that your body creates will bring sensuous allure to his back rub.

Reason #13   You haven't been sensuous lately: Let him know while you're making love that now you see things a little bit clearer. Be sure to mention that if he keeps it up you'll be able to regain your senses before he knows it. As you begin to come, whisper or yell out loud (it's up to you how loud), "I love what you do to me," or "I like the way you make me feel," or add your own to make it more personal.

Reason #14   You need some sensuous therapy: When he asks what he can do to make you feel better, suggest skinny dipping in the sauna, pool, shower, or tub. You can make it as fun and sexy as you want. One good thing to remember is if you're dipping in the bath-tub, make the water warm, add your favorite scents, get in, and re-lax with him.

Reason #15   You're cold: Tell him that making passionate love will lower the windchill factor by at least 60 percent.

Reason #16   You can make the earth move: Bet him two hours of head that you can make love to him and cause the earth to move.

Reason #17   You want to thank him for washing your hair last night: Reward him with a romantic picnic at your favorite park or lounge area.

Reason #18   Tell him that you know a winning lottery number: Add the number of climaxes that you and your lover experience in one week. Multiply this number by the size of your bed in inches. Once you hit the lottery, run out and buy *Will the Real Women . . . Please Stand Up!*

Reason #19   You want to discover the lost erogenous zone: Make plans to be the first to climax. If he climaxes before you, you owe him more sensuous sex. *Don't cheat!*

Reason # 20   Your sensuous fortune cookie told you to do it: Make up your own sensuous fortunes and place them wrapped on a spoon or fork handle each time you serve him a meal. He should read his fortune and follow the directions, then you read yours and follow the directions.

Reason #21   You decided not to do the laundry: Instead of doing the laundry, make passionate love to him.

❦ Making Love Better

Remember when you used to leap into each other's arms after only a few hours apart. The only thing that gets turned on now is the television. Sexual excitement has always been associated with naughtiness, badness, or dirtiness. All these elements are soon lost in sex that's too serious. When couples become committed to one another oftentimes sex soon becomes a job. What was once fun has become a hassle. Something that you once liked to do has become something you're supposed to do.

Remember the joyous *quickie*? Sexual enjoyment begins and ends with excitement, imagination, and playfulness. It means returning to the attitude that sex is fun, not a chore or a serious business governed by rules and other people's habits. Adopting an attitude of anything goes and what goes on tonight might not go on the next time can improve your love life. Allow yourselves to mix up the places where you have sex: in the bathroom, in the shower, in the living room. It's really up to you. Let your imagination soar (see Chapter 26, "Sexual Intercourse").

❦ Falling Out of Love

One of the unpleasant facts of life is falling out of love. Some women find it difficult to fall out of love. Despite all the mistreatment they suffered and all their insecurities, there is the possibility of being the fool. In most cases, you should be able to let bygones be gone. But what if he's the only man you want, the only man you feel you need. To rid yourself of this relationship, when you've had enough but can't let go, follow these simple steps:

1. List all your positive qualities on a piece of paper and post them on your mirror, in front of your toilet, or any place that you can see the list more than once a day.
2. Run a nice morning bath and close your eyes as you soak. Think of all your positive attributes and smile. Smile at the beginning of your new life.
3. As you step out of the tub, say his name once and when you say it use a belittling word to rhyme with his name such as:

Damn you Sam, Spoiled Carl. Be as unaffectionate as you can when you say his name. Mean what you say and say what you mean.

4. Write his name on a piece of paper. Gather up all the memorabilia that you have of him—shaving creams, pictures, colognes—and put them all in a bag and dump them in the trash. Remember that trash belongs in the trash.

5. Take cards, letters, or any writings and tear them up into small pieces. One by one toss the pieces in the toilet, the trash can, the trash compactor, and recite his name as negatively as you can. You are allowed to curse as you rid yourself of him. Good. Now, you've thrown away the emotional tie that you have to him.

6. Go out and buy a sexy new outfit and begin partying again, but don't pick out a man on the rebound. You can date, but don't fall in love too quickly or you'll be repeating these rituals again.

7. Don't look for a duplicate of the man you just split up with. Don't look for one with his features, build, or habits. Starting over means just that, and you've got to start over without him or any physical memories of him.

Do's and Don'ts of Ending Love

Do have the decency to tell him that it's over.

Don't give him the silent treatment and hope he'll get the message.

Don't write good-bye on the mirror in lipstick and think it's over.

Don't keep him on hold while you're trying to find a replacement.

Do give him equal time to express his feelings.

Don't pacify him by alluding to the possibility of getting back together.

Do be warm and friendly on the telephone.

Don't tease him when you know that you don't want him.

Don't suggest pairing him up with a friend.

Do invite him to a friend's party that you can't go to. This will give him a chance to meet new people.

Don't throw other prospects that you have in his face.
Don't continue to see him if you don't want him romantically.
Don't confront him if you see him with another woman.
Don't try to show up at the same place he is with another guy.

✸ *Healing After Breaking Up*

Healing from a broken relationship can be quite devastating, but you'll heal faster if you chart the stages from grief to rage to acceptance. The good thing about breaking up is that you lose weight, the bad thing is you cry all the time. When a relationship ends you come out of the cataclysm in stages. These stages are well defined. (According to a recent *New York Times* survey, it is usually the man who gets dumped.) No matter what the sex, people go through breakups in very similar ways.

Here's a nine-step path that most psychologists agree leads to healing:

1. *Bargaining:* With fate or God. You offer something to change in you to be a better person, let your hair grow out, lose weight, or give up smoking if he'll come back to you.
2. *Grieving:* Tightness of the chest, difficulty breathing, emotional numbness, feeling desperate and abandoned.
3. *Pain:* Anguish over the loss, a feeling of being deprived.
4. *Fear:* Night terrors and sweats; you feel that you will be alone forever.
5. *Sadness:* Deep sorrow that your life has led you to this point. You continue to say that your love affair could have worked or it almost worked.
6. *Anger:* Rage that you were not valued by your lover. Rage at the other woman. Rage about the circumstances that brought on the breakup.
7. *Depression:* Moping, feelings that you can't make the effort anymore, can't go through the trouble to date, can't make small talk with men.
8. *Acceptance:* The beginning of wellness. You begin to believe that you can and will survive without him. You appreciate what you had in the affair and understand that it's over.

9. *Hope and rebuilding:* You begin to take better care of yourself. You start to have a good time when you're on a date. You are eager to meet new people.

These stages are as predictable as the obstacles to happiness in a fairy tale, and, as in such tales, the going is far from easy. The three places where women I spoke with had the most trouble were grieving, anger, and acceptance.

Fantasies of happiness can sometimes overtake women. Making love and making dinner puts them on a natural high. In their words, the idea of keeping house is a turn-on to them, so they see this man in their lives as the ultimate satisfaction. Communication is difficult for women whose men have completely cut off. They therefore remain in the grieving stage. Grief doesn't care who it picks on, and it can also hurt the woman who did the leaving. Many people think it's easier to leave than to be left.

If you find it difficult or too painful to get over a lover, seeking professional help is best. If you find it impossible to reach out to your loved ones, then going for help is essential. If you're dysfunctional on your job or you're having trouble eating or sleeping, then you must get counseling and therapy. A physiological imbalance can be produced by deep internal reactions toward loss. Many women don't realize the shape they're in. That's why it's so important to know when you're past the normal stage of grief so help can be found. Accepting the end of an affair helps women to understand the part they played in the beginning as well as in the ending of it. Even if the breakup had not been their choice, they did accept and choose the man. Sometimes they may be less interested or even withdrawn in the affair. Women who are in these types of affairs tend to ignore the signs of pure rejection by making excuses for their man's lack of interest. When a woman makes her man her whole world or she becomes obsessed with him, she is opening herself up to heartbreak and anguish.

A breakup has a way of revealing emotional baggage to you. Start letting yourself in on your emotions and find out what you are subjecting yourself to, and then you can start to change your life. No matter how the style of loving changes, no matter how rough it appears or how heavy the load you appear to be carrying, the road to recovery after a breakup is the fact that you took another chance on love. Though wounded, you will heal. That's the positive news throughout this.

37

Contraceptives

The Pill, the condom, the diaphragm, Depo-Provera, Norplant, and sterilization—these are options available today for birth control. Women would like more information instead of new choices. Birth control is one of the major issues facing women in the nineties.

As fears of pregnancy and sexually transmitted diseases, including HIV, which causes AIDS, monopolize our thoughts, intelligent contraceptive selection is more important than ever before. Making that choice can be confusing no matter how sexually experienced a woman is. Here is *important* information on what you need to know about contraceptives: Before trying any contraceptives, be sure to check with your doctor for the best method for you.

◆◆ The Pill

Effectiveness: 94 to 97 percent
Used by: 10.8 million American women (31 percent of contraceptive users)
Cost: About $250 a year

The pill is the second most popular choice of birth control (after sterilization) in this country, and the one most often used by women aged fifteen to forty-four. It offers control over fertility, is easy to use, and is one of the most worry-free methods around. Pill users can expect regular periods with less bleeding, cramping, and premenstrual comfort. Risks are both ectopic pregnancy and pelvic inflammatory disease (PID), a potentially life-threatening condition. Pill use may reduce incidence of anemia, acne, and rheumatoid arthritis.

Protection against ovarian and endometrial cancers is probably the Pill's biggest advantage. Women who have used this method at any time during their lives have one fifth the chance of developing either of these diseases as do women who haven't. Cancer risk has sometimes decreased as length of use increased.

There are several disadvantages to oral-contraceptive use, including such hormone-related side effects as an altered menstrual cycle, headaches, nausea, weight change, and mood swings. The Pill is not recommended for women over thirty-five who smoke or for those with cardiovascular irregularities.

Pill users who decide they want to become pregnant are advised to switch to another form of birth control several months before trying to conceive.

⊕ The Condom

Effectiveness: 86 to 90 percent when used alone; 98 percent when combined with a spermicide
Used by: 5.2 million American women (15 percent of contraceptive users)
Cost: Approximately 50 cents per condom

The condom's main advantage, especially in recent years, is that it is the most effective of all contraceptives in preventing the spread of STD, and the only one known to impede the transmission of the AIDS virus. Condoms are also inexpensive and available without a prescription. Over half of all condoms are purchased by women.

Latex (rubber) condoms are the only kind that should be used if protection against STDs is a concern. (The more-porous lambskin types prevent pregnancy only.) Latex condoms differ in effectiveness: some are more prone to breakage and slippage than others. A wise choice is condoms lubricated with the spermicide nonoxynol-9. But no matter what type you use, always use a spermicide as a part of the procedure.

On the down side, some couples claim that condoms reduce spontaneity and sensation. Some women even report allergic reactions to latex.

❀ *The Diaphragm*

Effectiveness: 98 percent
Used by: 2 million American women (6 percent of contraceptive users)
Cost: $120 to $180 per year

Many women appreciate that the diaphragm is unobtrusive and, if inserted beforehand (up to six hours), does not affect spontaneity. Like other barrier methods, the diaphragm must be used with spermicidal jelly or cream. It provides some protection against STDs and PID.

Diaphragm use does, however, have a drawback, namely, an increased risk of urinary tract and bladder infections. Furthermore, spermicide must be reapplied each time you have sex, and allergic reactions to the spermicide or to the device itself are possible.

The diaphragm must be fitted by your doctor, and refitting may be required after weight loss or gain, childbirth, or pelvic surgery. Users should also be aware that the diaphragm is more likely to be dislodged in the female-on-top position.

❀ *The Depo-Provera Contraceptive Injection*

Effectiveness: More than 99 percent
Used by: 1½ to 2 million American women (5% of contraceptive users)
Cost: $31.71 per vial to health care providers

The Depo-Provera contraceptive injection was introduced in the United States in January 1993, although it has been in use in New

Zealand since 1969. More than 30 million women in 90 countries throughout the world are currently using this form of birth control.

Its almost total reliability and ease of use—one injection lasts three months—are its main advantages

Possible side effects are irregularity in the menstrual cycle, possible disappearance of menstruation altogether after one year of use (this will not affect fertility), and such other hormone-related side effects as headache, nausea, and potential weight gain.

❀ Foams, Creams, and Jellies

Effectiveness: 79 percent when used alone; up to 98 percent when used with a condom

Used by: 209,000 American women (0.6 percent of contraceptive users)

Cost: About $1.50 per application

Use of spermicidal foams, creams, or jellies offer some protection against STDs. Some products may not dissolve completely, however, increasing the risk of conception. Furthermore, all spermicides must be reapplied with each act of intercourse and users may experience more urinary tract infections than nonusers.

❀ The Intrauterine Device (IUD)

Effectiveness: 94 percent

Used by: 700,00 American women (2 percent of contraceptive users)

Cost: Approximately $90 for Progestasert, $300 for Copper T

Today's IUDs—progesterone-releasing Progestasert and copper-based Copper T—do not carry the same risks as their predecessor, the Dalkon Shield. Sold to more than 2.2 million women in the early seventies, the Shield has been blamed for pelvic infections resulting in infertility, devastating and prolonged pain, even death. The cause was thought to be a tail-string, used exclusively on the Shield, that drew bacteria from the vagina into the uterus.

Although Progestasert and the Copper T are definite improvements over the Dalkon Shield, they're far from risk free. Copper T users run twice the risk of pelvic infection as do women who use no contraception at all and they may suffer excessive bleeding and cramping. Ectopic pregnancy and infertility are other possible consequences. Of the two, Progestasert, which must be replaced annually (the Copper T can remain in place six years), is less likely to cause heavy menstrual flow and cramps, but its ectopic pregnancy rate is six to ten times higher than that of the Copper T.

❀ *The Cervical Cap*

Effectiveness: 87 to 98 percent
Used by: 40,000 American women (0.4 percent of contraceptive users)
Cost: $50 to $150

The cervical cap is the least popular of all forms of birth control. A close relative of the diaphragm, it provides forty-eight hours of protection without spermicide reapplication. It also helps prevent STDs.

A pap smear and a prescription are needed to obtain the cervical cap, which is harder to insert and easier to dislodge than the diaphragm. As a result, the failure rate may run as high as 25 percent for women under the age of thirty who have sex at least four times a week.

❀ *Norplant*

Effectiveness: 99.5 percent
Used by: 55,000 American women (in Food and Drug Administration testing only)
Cost: About $800, including doctor's fee, for up to five years of protection

The first major new contraceptive method to be approved by the Food and Drug Administration in nearly three decades, Norplant is a set of six matchsticklike progesterone-filled tubes that are inserted under the skin of the upper arm. This simple surgical procedure is done under local anesthesia in a doctor's office. Once in place, Norplant remains effective for up to five years, unless the user chooses to have it removed. Fertility is then immediately restored.

Because this method is so new, a limited number of doctors are currently trained to insert Norplant. Disadvantages include side effects similar to, although less severe than, those of the Pill: altered menstrual cycle, headaches, weight change, nausea. Their severity tends to lessen after six to nine months of use.

Norplant is also less effective in women who weigh more than 150 pounds and those with certain medical conditions—heart problems, liver disease, diabetes, high cholesterol, high blood pressure, breast cancer, or a history of blood clots—may not be good candidates for this method. Norplant is viewed as a long-term alternative to permanent sterilization.

❦ Sterilization

Effectiveness: Tubal ligation, 99.6 percent; vasectomy, 99.8 percent

Used by: 9.8 million American women and 4.2 million American men (40 percent of contraceptive users)

Cost: $1,500 to $2,500 for tubal ligation; $350 to $750 vasectomy

Besides being the only permanent method of contraception, sterilization is the sole nonbarrier method not tied to any long-term risks. Couples who choose sterilization must be absolutely certain they don't want any more children. As many as 70 percent of tubal ligations and 50 percent of vasectomies cannot be reversed.

Tubal ligation performed in a hospital under general anesthesia is considered major surgery but carries only slight risks of infection and other complications. No such risks exist for vasectomies, which are done under local anesthesia in a doctor's office. There has been an increase in the number of tubal ligations in recent years, which one study attributes to women opting for sterilization after having their IUDs removed.

Research is presently being conducted on a female vaccine that would produce antibodies against pregnancy. Three formulas are currently in development.

❧

If you want to enjoy life, keep living.

❧

38

AIDS: A Women's Issue

*U*ntil very recently, AIDS studies have concentrated only on the effects of HIV in men. The truth is now becoming clearer as women are accepting the facts and protecting themselves, because AIDS is a women's issue.

Dating several men; sleeping with them and not paying attention to the disease is one of the major reasons why women are contracting the AIDS virus. Young women worry about getting pregnant more than about getting AIDS.

Eleven years after its debut as a "gay man's disease," the AIDS epidemic has acquired a new face—female. Approximately 28,000 women have been reported with "full-blown" AIDS and approximately 150,000 more are likely to be infected with HIV, the virus that causes AIDS. Symptoms of life-threatening AIDS don't develop until about five years after being infected.

African-American women make up about half of all the cases and Hispanic women about one fifth. These numbers, however, don't tell the complete story, because it doesn't tell about the women who are infected with HIV but do not have "full-blown"

AIDS. These women have certain symptoms that include cancer of the cervix, pelvic infections, vaginal yeast infections, pneumonia, and tuberculosis. Women have died because of these diseases, but they have never been counted as victims of the deadly disease. Despite evidence that some of these diseases are more common and severe in women infected with HIV, gynecological disorders or cancers were not listed as a part of AIDS-defining infections. The Centers for Disease Control and Prevention (CDC) have been reluctant to add these conditions because they also infect women without HIV. The CDC upgraded its AIDS definition to include invasive cervical cancer and low blood levels of CD4 cells. These cells help to fight infections and low blood levels increase a person's risk of developing diseases.

The number of women recognized as having AIDS has steadily risen, and will continue to rise over the next decade. New additions by the CDC to the AIDS definition have helped to create this boost in numbers. The AIDS infection accounted for 37 percent of all cases of AIDS in women in 1991. According to the CDC, the number of heterosexually acquired AIDS cases in general has jumped 25 percent each year from 1989 to 1992.

❧ Susceptibility of Women to AIDS

The rapid rise of AIDS in women, and the fact that women are at least ten times more susceptible to contracting HIV during intercourse than men, occurs for several reasons. Women are much more vulnerable because of the high concentration of the virus in semen than in vaginal fluid. It is also possible for the virus of the infected semen to slip easily into a woman's body by way of vaginal sores from other sexually transmitted diseases or tiny cuts and tears found in the vagina or labia.

Research into AIDS prevention and treatment strategies for women have been slowed by the government. Some women health advocates have used this fact as part of the blame for the current women's AIDS epidemic in this country. The false accusations that women who fostered the virus were prostitutes, promiscuous, or IV drug users led the government to disregard any other women as being in the HIV path. The alarm was not sounded soon enough and now more women are at risk for getting AIDS. Anyone can get

AIDS. You do not have to sleep with several men to get AIDS, noted Charles C. J. Carpenter, M.D., professor of medicine at Brown University. Many women with AIDS who acquire it heterosexually were seeing only one man when they contacted the virus. Many of these women had sexual relationships with men who didn't even know they had the virus. Many men who carry the virus keep it to themselves while continuing to have intercourse with women or wives without using condoms.

❦ You Must Protect Yourself

There are many things that you can do as a woman to protect yourself. The standard AIDS-prevention questions to ask your partner are:

1. Have you had a positive AIDS test?
2. Have you had sex with multiple partners recently or other men?
3. Have you used intravenous drugs?
4. Have you engaged in sexual practices where the skin was broken during sex?
5. Have you had unprotected sex?
6. Have you had a blood transfusion?

If he answers yes to any of these questions, he's at risk of having the AIDS virus. Of course, there is no guarantee that a man will answer these questions truthfully. He may not know that he has slept with an infected person, or he may not want you to know that he is carrying the virus. In addition to this is the fact that the virus can take up to six months to show up on a test. It is therefore absolutely essential to practice safe sex unless you are certain that he has been faithful, or he has been tested for the virus and retested every six months.

Practicing safe sex is sometimes difficult, but there are ways to protect yourself. Using the latex condom is the only weapon available at this time, besides abstinence. Studies have shown that the use of condoms have been highly effective at preventing the spread of HIV. Many men refuse to use condoms and women sometimes submit to their lover's requests by making love without using a condom.

Here are a few sensuous ways to effectively slip a condom onto your lover's penis.

1. Be as erotic as possible about using condoms.
2. Offer to put it on for him, and as you put it on him massage his penis sensuously. There's no need to be afraid to do it because it's for your own safety.
3. Be sure to add lubricants that are water based such as K-Y Jelly. Vaseline corrodes condoms, so don't use it.
4. Try using colorful or textured condoms to add variety.
5. Use the condom as the avenue to turn him on.
6. Have healthy love play by discussing condoms with your lover or even members of your family. Surprisingly, many women lack interest in their own health priority.

Many women tend to take care of everyone in the family, but forget to take care of themselves.

⚜

Get physically involved with your community.

⚜

Conclusion

As I conclude this book, I would like to share my own personal convictions on what I believe to be the source of correct sexual principles. I believe that correct sexual principles are whatever feels most natural to you and whatever contributes to your overall happiness. I believe that as women mature they can learn to be real—that is, they learn to make wiser decisions in life and in love.

Your decision to become a Real Woman will express your personal quest for inner and outer beauty, for your own courage, and your love for human nature. You will discover that you must never lose your desire to explore and to experiment with new methods of improving yourself and your sexuality. By exploring your sensuous side, you will arrive at a point where you begin to discover your own capabilities, thus increasing your ability to do what it takes to create an effective and exciting life for you and your mate. You will then learn what it is to be true to yourself. You will be a woman who is adored, respected, and appreciated. But first and foremost, you must respect yourself. That is the first principle of being a Real Woman.

Index

About the Author

Ella Patterson is an entrepreneur, sex educator, self-published author, and professional speaker extraordinaire. She is founder and CEO of Knowledge Concepts Educational Systems, a motivational company dedicated to informing and inspiring women to accept their sexuality in wholesome, positive, and nurturing ways. With degrees (B.S.) in both biology and health education, she taught in the Dallas Independent School District for fourteen years. She lives outside of Dallas, Texas, with her husband and son.

For more information on Knowledge Concepts Educational Systems, Inc., or any Ella Patterson companies or products, call toll free 1-800-269-6228, or send in the coupon below.

RETURN TO:

Knowledge Concepts Educational Systems, Inc. (KCES)
P. O. Box 973
Cedar Hill, Texas 75104
or Phone: toll free 1-800-269-6228
Please send me information on KCES, Inc., lectures, seminars, workshops or products.

NAME (*please print*)

PHONE (*business*)　　　　　　　　　　PHONE (*home*)

ADDRESS

CITY　　　　　　　　STATE　　　　　　　ZIP

Use ball point pen only.